300
TIPS
for
PAINTING &
DECORATING

300
TIPS
for
PAINTING &
DECORATING

Tips, Techniques & Trade Secrets

Alison Jenkins

FIREFLY BOOKS

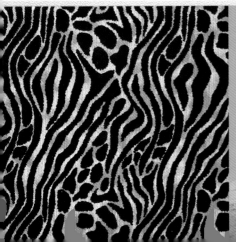

A FIREFLY BOOK

Published by Firefly Books Ltd. 2014

First printing

Publisher Cataloging-in-Publication Data (U.S.)

Jenkins, Alison.
300 tips for painting and decorating : tips, techniques and trade secrets /
Alison Jenkins.
[176] pages : col. photos. ; cm.
Includes index.
Summary: Tools, equipment and preparation for painting interior walls, ceilings, doors and windows.
ISBN-13: 978-1-77085-452-9 (pbk.)
1. Interior painting. 2. Interior decoration. I. Title.
II. Three hundred tips for painting and decorating.
698.14 dc 23 TT323.J454 2014

Library and Archives Canada Cataloguing in Publication

Jenkins, Alison, author
        300 tips for painting & decorating : tips, techniques & trade secrets / Alison Jenkins.
Includes index.
ISBN 978-1-77085-452-9 (pbk.)
        1. House painting – Amateurs' manuals. 2. Interior decoration – Amateurs' manuals. 3. Decoration and ornament – Amateurs' manuals.
I. Title. II. Title: Three hundred tips for painting and decorating.
III. Title: Painting & decorating.
TT323.J45 2014   698'.14   C2014-901441-4

Published in the United States by
Firefly Books (U.S.) Inc.
P.O. Box 1338, Ellicott Station
Buffalo, New York 14205

Published in Canada by
Firefly Books Ltd.
50 Staples Avenue, Unit 1
Richmond Hill, Ontario L4B 0A7

Color separation by Pica Digital Pte Ltd, Singapore
Printed in China by 1010 Printing International Ltd

Conceived, designed and produced by
Quarto Publishing plc
The Old Brewery
6 Blundell Street
London N7 9BH

QUAR.TFID

FOR QUARTO
Project editor **Chelsea Edwards**; Art editor **Jackie Palmer**; Designers **Jackie Palmer, Simon Brewster**; Illustrator: **Kuo Kang Chen**; Photographer **Philip Wilkins**; Picture researcher **Sarah Bell**; Copyeditor **Liz Jones**; Proofreader **Michelle Pickering**; Indexer **Helen Snaith**; Art director **Caroline Guest**; Creative director **Moira Clinch**; Publisher **Paul Carslake**

contents

Chapter 3:
Walls, ceilings and floors 64

Foreword

My passion for home decorating grew from a childhood love of paint and paper and a fascination with making things out of anything that I could find. The purchase of my first small apartment and the subsequent shortage of the necessary funds to carry out decorations and repairs reminded me of something my mother used to say: "If you want something done, do it yourself!" I decided to do just that and embarked on a DIY and home-decorating learning curve that resulted in the lovely home I'd envisaged, without breaking the bank.

Doing your own home decorating provides the ultimate opportunity for self-expression. You have the chance to create a living space that reflects your lifestyle and personality, and the ability to be spontaneous if you change your mind and want to try something new. And that's why I love it!

I hope you enjoy this book, whether you're a complete novice or a more seasoned home decorator; perhaps home decoration will become your passion, too.

Alison Jenkins

About this book

Split into five chapters, this book guides you through compiling a suitable toolkit and preparing for the task at hand, before addressing individual elements of home decoration. Whether you're looking for what to put on your walls, ceilings or floors or want to focus on windows and doors, there's a dedicated section you can consult. Easy-to-follow step-by-step instructions for painting, papering, tiling and key maintenance tasks that make your home run smoothly are all featured. These pages are packed with ideas, information and images of inspirational interiors that will whet your appetite and fill you with the confidence you need to go ahead and "do it yourself." In addition, the "TRY IT" and "FIX IT" panels let you in on all those little tips, tricks and secrets to make home decoration easy, quick and most importantly ... fun!

How-to sequences
The best or most efficient way to do things is explained every step of the way.

Try-it panels
These suggest new approaches to decorating that you may not have previously considered.

Tips
Each collection of tips reveals practical information to help you achieve the result you want.

Fix-it panels
Correct mistakes or avoid them altogether with these invaluable nuggets of advice.

Diagrams
Helpful diagrams are used to reveal what a photograph can't show.

Ideas
Photographs of wonderful interiors provide ideas aplenty.

Analysis
Images are contextualized and analyzed so you can re-create the look.

1

Tools, equipment and materials

Novice home decorators might be overwhelmed by the amount of equipment and the range of materials featured in this chapter. However, the idea is to build a collection of tools over time (sometimes a lifetime!) as and when the need arises. Start with the essential kit, then make new purchases according to the decorating task you've chosen to undertake. Remember, a piece of equipment is useless unless you know how to use it and what to use it for; this chapter will tell you everything you need to know about home decoration tools and materials.

Recessed carrying handle on lid

Small, sealable compartments for screws/nails, etc.

Toolbox

A well-organized, well-stocked toolbox is surely a wonder to behold. However, any experienced DIY enthusiast will tell you that it takes many years to accumulate a comprehensive collection of tools, equipment and all of the other bits and pieces necessary to cope with all eventualities. The rule is to begin with the basics and add to your collection as you need to.

Inner tray lifts out for easy accessibility

Carrying handle

Sturdy catches

TRY IT

Keep your toolbox dry

Cut a piece of cardboard to fit inside the base of your toolbox. The card will absorb any moisture that may build up inside the box and will help to keep your tools dry and in good condition. This is useful if you generally keep your toolbox in a garage or outdoor storage area. The cardboard can be replaced with a new piece when it gets damp.

Compartments in the toolbox lid are useful for keeping drill bits handy.

1   Choosing a toolbox

In order to keep your tools organized and readily available you will need a suitable container. You will see a dazzling array of tool containers in DIY stores, in all shapes and sizes with price tags to match. To begin with, choose one that will accommodate your basic toolbox (see page 14) with space for a few extras. Remember, bigger is not always better, as an enormous toolbox will be unwieldy and cumbersome. You can always upgrade to a larger toolbox when your collection expands, and that way you may end up with a "static" tool store for larger items and a smaller portable one to keep by your side as you work. Most toolboxes have a lift-out tray with compartments to hold bits, screws, small hand tools and other useful items. The tray can be handy to keep close by when working on a project so you don't lose anything. The color and style of the toolbox is of course a matter of personal preference.

Cantilevered toolboxes allow access to all compartments at once when fully open, then fold away neatly when not in use.

An example of a "static" toolbox; plenty of storage space but too heavy to carry around!

2 Helping with heights

A tool belt can be invaluable if your home-decorating task requires the use of a ladder. Simply tuck the tools you need for the job into the tool belt then you won't have to keep coming down to the toolbox to get what you need. However, a tool belt can be cumbersome and heavy if overloaded.

3 Top toolbox tips

- Use small sealable plastic bags for keeping similar items together – screws, nails, bits and so on.

- Try not to overload your toolbox so you can easily locate the tool you need.

- Empty and vacuum the box occasionally, as dirt and grit can damage blades.

- In order to keep your tools in good condition, occasionally use a soft cloth to rub them with a little oil. Good-quality, well-cared-for tools can last a lifetime.

- Try to keep your tool collection together. There's nothing more frustrating than not being able to find what you need, when you need it.

- Consider starting a "tool pool" with your friends and like-minded DIY enthusiasts to share items that you may only need once or twice; this saves money.

- Safety note – it is always advisable to store bladed tools inside a toolbox in order to prevent accidents.

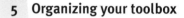

4 Hardware storage boxes

These are really handy if you have lots of different screws, nails and other small bits and pieces. However, it's easy to get confused, so make sure to label the drawers so you know what's inside.

5 Organizing your toolbox

In general it's a good idea to keep the tools you use most frequently at the top of the box or in the upper compartments, and place the ones you don't use so much in the bottom. An open tool tote is also very useful for taking along to the work site; simply fill it with the tools required for the job.

TRY IT

Ready-made tool kit

If you really don't know where to start, then you can't go wrong with a ready-assembled toolbox. Most DIY stores will have plenty to choose from and will contain most of the essentials. They're a good gift idea for a new homeowner, or a budding DIY enthusiast.

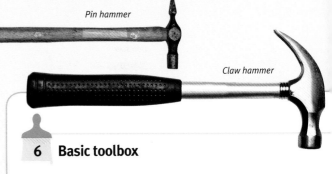

Pin hammer

Claw hammer

Hand tools

Hand tools are powered by elbow grease rather than household electricity or a battery. A basic toolbox is something that no home should be without – you never know when you might need to hang a picture, tighten the screws in a door handle or fix a wobbly chair. Here you can find out exactly what equipment to keep in the toolbox, why you need it and how to choose it so that you are fully equipped and prepared to deal with most DIY tasks.

6 Basic toolbox

- **Hammers** Two will suffice: a 16 oz or 20 oz claw hammer and a lightweight pin hammer. The former drives in nails, and the claw part is used as a lever to pry nails out again. The latter is useful when you are using smaller nails or fine panel nails.

- **Screwdriver set** Look for a starter set that includes a few flat-bladed and cross-head (Phillips) screwdrivers in different sizes. Add to your collection as you progress through your home-decoration tasks.

- **Plier set** These are usually available as a matching set of three with insulated handles: flat-nosed, long-nosed and a side cutter. The first two are used for any kind of job that requires a firmer and more secure gripping action than your fingers are capable of, while the side cutter is useful for snipping off ends of wire.

- **Adjustable wrench** Use this tool as a substitute for a full set of open-ended wrenches. The adjustable jaws will fit most nut heads.

- **Hex keys** Most flatpack furniture arrives with its own hex (or Allen) tool for assembly; however, these do tend to get lost so keep a set at hand for minor adjustments.

- **Utility knife** Buy a utility knife with a comfortable grip and a retractable blade. Use it for cutting, trimming and scoring. Use with a steel rule for straight cuts, and always take care not to cut your fingers.

- **Junior hacksaw** This is a small steel-framed saw that has a replaceable blade and is used for cutting metal (pipes, bolts) and also plastic (curtain track) and narrow timber (dowels, battens).

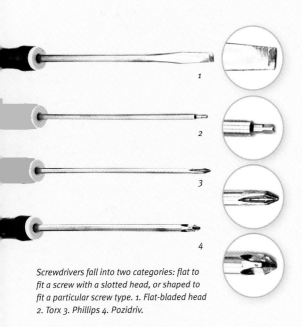

1

2

3

4

Screwdrivers fall into two categories: flat to fit a screw with a slotted head, or shaped to fit a particular screw type. 1. Flat-bladed head 2. Torx 3. Phillips 4. Pozidriv.

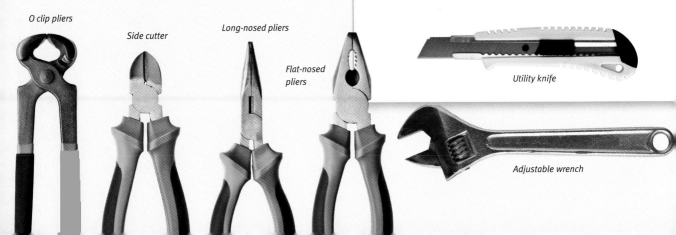

O clip pliers

Side cutter

Long-nosed pliers

Flat-nosed pliers

Utility knife

Adjustable wrench

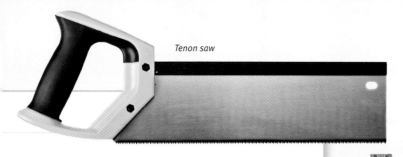

Tenon saw

7 How to buy hand tools

- Try before you buy, if possible. For example, does that hammer feel good in your hand – is it too heavy, too lightweight? If you cannot use a tool comfortably then it does not deserve its place in your toolbox.

- Look for starter sets of tools such as screwdrivers, pliers and wrenches – this is cheaper than buying individual items. You can buy add-ons later.

- Multi tools can be useful. Look for screwdrivers with interchangeable bits. This saves space in the toolbox, too.

- If you don't need it, don't buy it. Think about the task ahead, then purchase any additional tools required to complete the job.

- **Tenon saw** A small saw with a rigid blade, used for making straight cuts in timber.

- **Try square** This is used to mark and measure a right angle. It's useful when making straight cuts across pieces of wood, or for checking interior or exterior angles when assembling flatpack furniture.

- **Steel tape measure** Most domestic decoration jobs will require measuring in some form. Buy a retractable steel tape measure that is at least 10 ft (3 m) long, with both imperial and metric markings. Most have a locking mechanism, which is useful if you're working alone without a friend to hold the other end of the tape.

- **Spirit level** Used to indicate true horizontal and vertical planes, which is important when putting up shelves or hanging wallpaper. Place the level on the plane and make adjustments so the indicator bubble rests between the markings in the vial.

- **Steel ruler** A metal ruler is a better item for your toolbox than a plastic one, because it won't scratch or break. Also, a metal ruler can be used with your utility knife. A standard 12 in (30 cm) ruler is fine for most jobs; invest in a longer one if necessary.

- **Bradawl** An indispensable item, most useful for making pilot holes in materials prior to drilling screw holes. Making a pilot hole in wood can reduce the chance of it splitting.

- **Nail punch** A steel tool with a small cup-shaped recess at the pointed end. This is used together with a hammer to drive nail heads just below the surface so the recess may be filled, rendering the nail invisible.

- **Pencils** A few pencils are useful for marking out and measuring. HB grades are ideal as they are quite robust and do not leave a very dark mark.

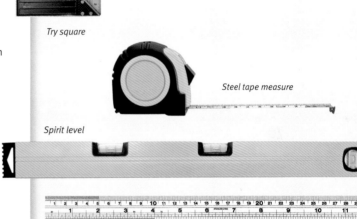

Try square

Steel tape measure

Spirit level

Steel ruler

Bradawl

Nail punch

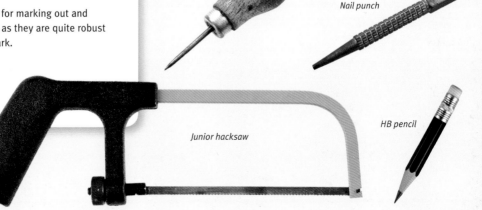

Junior hacksaw

HB pencil

Hex keys

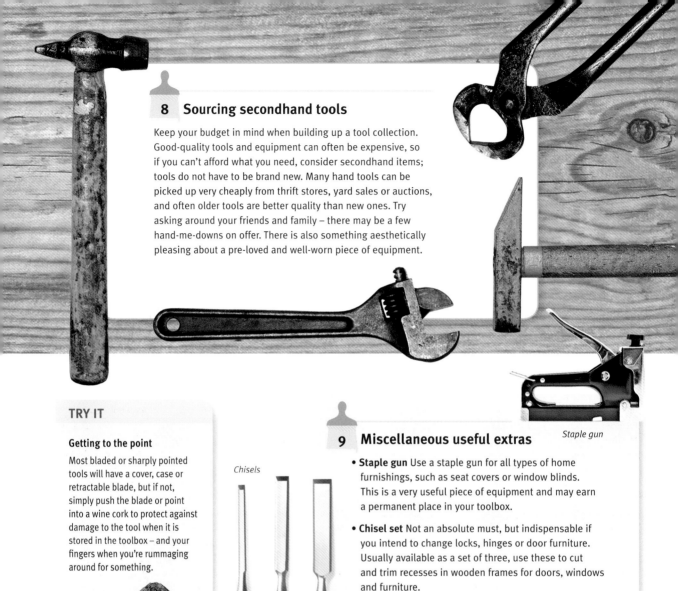

8 Sourcing secondhand tools

Keep your budget in mind when building up a tool collection. Good-quality tools and equipment can often be expensive, so if you can't afford what you need, consider secondhand items; tools do not have to be brand new. Many hand tools can be picked up very cheaply from thrift stores, yard sales or auctions, and often older tools are better quality than new ones. Try asking around your friends and family – there may be a few hand-me-downs on offer. There is also something aesthetically pleasing about a pre-loved and well-worn piece of equipment.

TRY IT

Getting to the point

Most bladed or sharply pointed tools will have a cover, case or retractable blade, but if not, simply push the blade or point into a wine cork to protect against damage to the tool when it is stored in the toolbox – and your fingers when you're rummaging around for something.

Chisels

Staple gun

9 Miscellaneous useful extras

- **Staple gun** Use a staple gun for all types of home furnishings, such as seat covers or window blinds. This is a very useful piece of equipment and may earn a permanent place in your toolbox.

- **Chisel set** Not an absolute must, but indispensable if you intend to change locks, hinges or door furniture. Usually available as a set of three, use these to cut and trim recesses in wooden frames for doors, windows and furniture.

- **Flashlight** A small flashlight is handy in case you have a power cut or need a little illumination in the attic, the basement, under the floorboards or in a dark cupboard.

- **Surform plane** A handheld sander that looks similar to a Parmesan cheese grater. Used for shaping, rounding off cut timber edges and making quick fixes like paring down a door that binds in its frame.

- **Duct tape** General, all-purpose, strong sticky stuff useful for all sorts of temporary fixing and repairing, and also for holding down trailing cables while you work.

Flashlight

Surform plane

Duct tape

Power tools

Power tools will save you a great deal of time and energy. Both corded and cordless power tools can be expensive, so it's worthwhile to consider the type of home decorator you are and then choose your tools accordingly. Here are the top three power tools, plus some suggestions for other items that might lighten the DIY load.

11 Power tool safety

Power tools have rotating bits, cutting blades, sanding plates, gears and all sorts of rapidly moving parts that may cause injury. Always engage the safety guard if there is one, and never place hands or fingers where they may accidentally come into contact with sharp points, blades or abrasive surfaces.

10 Top three power tools

DRILL/DRIVER

A power drill/driver – either corded or cordless (or both, if you're really keen) – is without a doubt the most useful tool to have at your disposal. Use as a drill to make clearance holes and countersunk recesses for screws, or as a screwdriver to drive in and remove screws. Versatile and invaluable, this tool is a must for all home improvement projects.

Look for these features:
- Variable speed settings for greater control (1)
- Keyless chuck (2)
- Forward and reverse action (3)
- Clutch settings for driving screws (4)
- Comfortable hand grip (5)

SANDER

If you have ever sanded anything by hand, then you will know that it is hard work, even on a small area. Sanding and finishing are probably the most frequently performed home-decorating tasks, whether simply smoothing off the cut end of a wooden batten, or finishing off filled surface imperfections in a wall before applying paint or paper.

Look for these features:
- Dust bag attachment (1)
- Quick fit and replace sanding sheets (2)

JIGSAW

A jigsaw (or saber saw) cuts timber and board up to 2 in (50 mm) in thickness; different blades are available for cutting plastic, metal and ceramic materials. The short blade is powered vertically through a base plate and can be used for straight and curved cuts. Some models have an adjustable tilting base plate, for cutting angles; this is handy for cutting accurate miters in base boards, chair or picture rails.

Look for these features:
- Adjustable base plate (1)
- Variable speed control (2)
- Dust bag attachment (3)
- Locking device (4)
- Easy blade change facility (5)

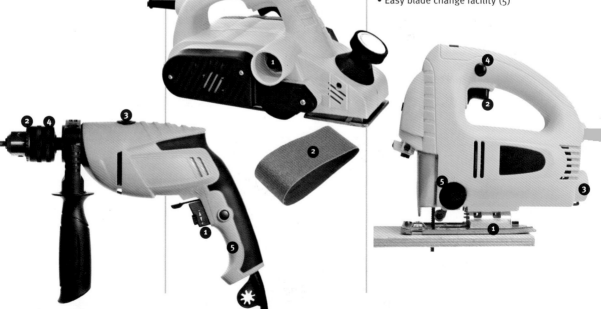

12   Power tool buying tips

- If you are likely to be an occasional user, buy domestic tools as opposed to heavier duty, more expensive professional models.

- If you don't recognize the brand name, do some research online before purchase.

- Only buy good-quality tools; cheaper alternatives may be a false economy.

- See if the tool includes extra blades or attachments – or are they purchased separately?

- Compare features between brands – are there several commonalities or specialized features that set one brand above the rest?

- Check that the store has a return policy for power tools, as well as offers a guarantee.

- Does the tool come with a carrying case?

13   Corded vs. cordless

In general corded tools are considered more powerful than cordless versions, but due to technical innovations in battery design that is changing fast. The main points to consider are power versus convenience. Are you going to be up a ladder putting up shelves or curtain tracks, or embarking on a job that requires a long run time and high power? Use the chart as a guide to help you decide which kind you need.

CORDED	CORDLESS
• Household powered, no recharging required. • Best for long, high-intensity jobs with little or no downtime.	• Battery powered, will need regular recharging. • Long periods of non-use will shorten battery life. • Additional batteries can be expensive.
• Generally more powerful than cordless.	• Generally less powerful than corded.
• Work area restricted to length of cable, unless used with an extension cable. • Cables can be a trip hazard.	• Portable and convenient. • Useful where there is no convenient power source, in high-traffic areas or when working aloft.
• Single unit.	• Some cordless tools can be purchased as a set with several tools sharing one or two battery packs.
• Full range of tools available.	• Not all tools are available as a cordless version.

14   Know your sander types

Belt or sheet sander	Takes rectangular sanding sheets and is most useful for finishing large areas, planed wood and smooth boards.
Orbital sander	Sanding plate moves in a circular orbit (regular or random, depending on the model), suitable for general sanding and finishing.
Detail sander	Has a shaped sanding plate that takes pointed or triangular sanding sheets. Useful for finishing tight corners and awkward areas. Detail sanders are available in a small palm size too.

Belt sander

Sheet orbital sander

Random orbital sander

Detail sander

15 A useful extra

A cordless screwdriver is small enough to keep in the toolbox. This power tool has a set of flat- and cross-head bits to choose from, useful for flatpack construction and working in tight spaces.

17 Corded power tool safety

The cable attached to a power tool can easily be damaged through misuse or general wear and tear. Never carry or suspend a power tool by the cord or pull the cord to disengage it from the power supply. Do not use a tool that has a damaged plug or frayed cord; replace or have the tool professionally repaired or serviced.

TRY IT

Power tool helpful hints

- Allow an electric drill to cool down during extended periods of use in order to avoid overheating.
- When using a jigsaw, allow the motor to reach full speed before engaging with the work piece.
- Keep your sander dust free; accumulation of grime and fine dust particles can cause overheating. Use a paintbrush to remove dust after use.

16 Bits and blades

It is good practice when buying a power tool to ensure that you have also purchased blades/bits to go with it; some tools have a starter set provided, and some do not. Use the chart as a guide to help you decide which kind you need.

Top to bottom: coarse, medium and fine jigsaw blades

DRILL BITS	JIGSAW BLADES
• Twist drill bits for wood and metal; sets range in size from 1–10 mm. • Countersink bits – for recessing clearance holes. • Masonry bits – for solid walls (6, 7 and 8 mm are most useful). • Screwdriver bits – a double-ended bit or a set of flat- and cross-head bits. • Spade bits – for making large holes in wood. • Tile bits – for drilling ceramic tiles.	• Coarse, medium and fine wood-cutting blades. Also useful for cutting plastic and other sheet materials. • Blade with finer teeth for making smooth cuts in metal. • Specialty ceramic blades for tile cutting.

Ceramic jigsaw blade

Coarse wood-cutting jigsaw blade

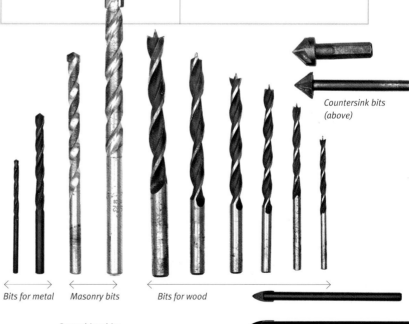

Countersink bits (above)

Bits for metal   *Masonry bits*   *Bits for wood*

Screwdriver bits

Tile bits (above)

Changeable heads

Spade bit

Decorating kit

It is surprising how much equipment is required for basic decorating – however, most items are readily available and relatively inexpensive. If you have a little flexibility in your budget it is worth investing in good-quality paintbrushes; rollers and paint pads are fairly disposable, but if used and cared for correctly a good set of paintbrushes will last a lifetime.

Handrail

Tool shelf (do not stand on this!)

An aluminum ladder is a good choice for the home decorator as it is lightweight and easy to carry around. It can also be stored on wall hooks in the garage or utility room when not in use.

Locking spreader bars or cords

Non-slip safety feet

18 Must-have: access equipment

Unless you are very tall or have extremely low ceilings, you will need a ladder of some sort. A lightweight aluminum folding stepladder will be perfectly adequate for basic decorating – choose one that has seven treads and a tray at the top to hold your paint or other tools. See page 103 for other access combinations, for example if you're decorating a stairwell or papering ceilings.

19 Preparation essentials

- **Drop/dust cloths** Never begin a decorating job without first protecting any floor areas with drop cloths. These can be made of cotton or plastic and will save your floorcoverings from paint splashes or sticky paper residue.

- **Scraper** A knife with a wide, flat, flexible blade, used for removing old wallcoverings or paint without damaging the surface below.

- **Filling knife** Similar to a scraper, but with a narrower blade, used for applying filler.

- **Shave hook** A tool with a shaped blade set at right angles to the handle; the differently shaped edges are really useful for removing paint from moldings on window frames or furniture.

- **Wallpaper stripper** A steam wallpaper stripper will make light work of removing old wallcoverings.

- **Heat gun** Looks like a hairdryer, and is not essential but really useful for removing paint from woodwork. It emits hot air that gently melts the paint, facilitating easy removal using a shave hook or scraper.

Shave hook

Wallpaper stripper

Scraper

Filling knife

Heat gun

20 Basic painting kit

Most painting jobs can be accomplished with a few basic tools, and every home decorator has their favorite application method. A combination of methods is usually the most successful.

TOOL	APPLICATIONS	PROS	CONS
Brush	Small brushes for woodwork, larger brushes for flat areas.	• Easy to use and clean. • Range of sizes readily available.	• Tiring to apply paint to a large area using a brush. • Watch out for drips.
Roller	Walls or ceilings.	• Easy to use. • Fast paint application.	• Considerable paint wastage. • Clean-up process is time-consuming. • Can splatter if overloaded.
Paint pad	General wall and ceiling painting.	• Fast and easy application. • Minimum wastage. • Easy to clean.	• Not so effective on woodwork.

TRY IT

Decanting paint

If you have bought paint in a large can or container it makes sense to decant a little into a paint pail for ease of portability when painting small areas with a brush. Paint pails have a handle that can be suspended from a ladder with a hook.

21 Natural, synthetic or foam?

Natural bristles	Considered an investment purchase, as they can be expensive. Can leave brush marks if overloaded; a little practice is necessary to produce good results. Will last a long time if cared for correctly. Tend to improve with age. May shed a few bristles when new.
Synthetic fiber bristles	Relatively inexpensive, and molt-free. Polyester and nylon mixtures perform better than nylon bristles. Easy to handle and clean.
Foam	Inexpensive enough to be disposable and are available in a variety of sizes. Do not leave brush marks and are most suitable for touch-up jobs.

22 Three key paintbrushes

You will need a selection of brushes in different sizes to start with, and then you can add to your collection as and when required.

- 4 in (100 mm) for walls and ceilings

- 1 in (25 mm) for woodwork

- ½ in (13 mm) straight or angled brush for cutting in

23 Roller or pad?

Rollers are available in two standard widths: 7 in
(178 mm) and 9 in (229 mm). Choose a sturdy roller
with a wire cage construction and a paint tray to match.
A long-handled mini roller is used to paint behind radiators or
pipework or in small, awkward spaces. Roller sleeves can be
made of long- or short-pile fleece or foam. Choose short-pile or
foam for smooth surfaces, and a longer pile for surfaces that are
uneven or textured. When painting ceilings or high walls, use an
extension handle fitted to the paint roller handle, which will
enable you to paint without the use of a ladder.

   Paint pads are most readily available as a kit containing a
paint tray, a wall pad, a smaller pad for woodwork and a narrow
detail pad. The tray has a reservoir for paint and a loading
system for the foam pad.

*Long-pile
standard roller*

24 Using a new roller?

New rollers with a long pile
have a tendency to shed fibers,
which will spoil your paint
finish. Run a lint roller over the
pile to remove loose fibers,
then rinse the roller sleeve in
water and allow to dry out
completely before using.

Large paint pad

*Set of foam touch-
up brushes*

*Long-handled
mini roller*

Mini roller and paint tray

TRY IT

Power painting

If you have very large areas
to paint, a battery/electrically
powered paint delivery system may
save you time, as you don't have to keep
reloading the roller. The unit can be
carried as a backpack or placed on the
floor, and the paint is delivered from a
reservoir through a hose to the roller.

25 Painting hard-to-reach areas

Long-length mini rollers are great for getting to
hard-to-reach places such as behind radiators.
If you prefer to use a paint pad, you can use
duct tape to fix a thin length of wooden batten
to the handle of your normal paint pad to
extend the reach and save the expense of
buying a separate paint pad.

Plumb line

Bucket

26 Wallpapering kit

Wallpapering is not really difficult, but it can be tricky at first. The right tools and equipment make the job a lot easier.

- **Bucket** A simple plastic bucket in which to mix up the wallpaper paste.

- **Wallpaper paste** Available in powder form to be mixed with water. Also available ready-mixed for sticking borders, friezes and loose edges.

- **Tape measure and pencil** To measure and mark the lengths of wallpaper.

- **Paper-hanging scissors** With extra-long blades, just right for cutting and trimming wallpaper.

- **Wallpapering table** Relatively inexpensive folding wallpapering tables are a must when pasting. They fold away for neat storage when not in use.

- **Pasting brush** Use a large pasting brush for applying paste to the paper; most have a hook on the handle so you can hang them on the edge of the bucket.

- **Plumb line** Use this to mark a vertical line from ceiling to floor as a guide for hanging the first lengths.

- **Paper-hanging brush** A wide brush used to smooth the paper into place. You can use a large sponge instead if using washable wallpaper.

- **Seam roller** A small handheld tool that is run along the joins between paper lengths to make sure the edges are firmly adhered to the wall.

- **Sugar soap (or trisodium phosphate)** Available as powder mixed with water, or ready-mixed; use it to wash down walls before decorating.

- **Size** Used as a sealant for stripped walls or new finishes such as plaster or drywall. Makes the surface less absorbent and therefore easier to paper.

Seam roller

Pasting brushes

Scissors

Sugar soap

Wallpaper paste

Wallpapering table

TRY IT

Prevent your paper curling

Tie a length of string between the legs of your wallpapering table at one end. You can tuck the end of the paper under the string to keep it from curling up while you apply the paste.

Decorating sundries

Or in other words – sandpaper. When you are painting and decorating, a professional result depends on adequate surface preparation, and that means sanding down to a smooth finish after stripping or filling, and before applying paint or paper. The type and grade will depend on the material and surface to be worked; use these guides to inform your choice.

TRY IT

Sanding curves

Flexible sanding sponges make light work of contoured surfaces like wooden moldings on door or window frames. Sponges are available in different grades and can be rinsed to remove dust residue, then reused.

27 Know your sandpaper grades

The word "grit" simply refers to the number of abrasive particles the abrasive sheet has per inch; the higher the grit number, the more particles per inch and vice versa. Low numbers indicate coarse paper and, as the number increases, so does the fineness.

GRIT	NAME	APPLICATIONS
40–60	Coarse	Sanding and stripping away paint and smoothing out large surface imperfections. Roughing up surfaces to create a good key.
80–120	Medium	Smoothing out minor surface imperfections.
150–180	Fine	Final stages of surface finishing.
Up to 600	Extra fine	Used for very fine finishing between paint/varnish coats; not commonly used for general decorating work.
Various grades available	Wet-and-dry paper	Used with water or other lubricants for sanding metals and plastics that are unsuitable for use with dry papers.

Coarse

Medium

Fine

TRY IT

FOLD A SQUARE SHEET OF SANDPAPER TO MAXIMIZE SURFACE USE
This method extends the life of the paper when hand sanding. When the grit on one surface has been worn away, simply refold to reveal a fresh plane ready for use. If you require a smaller size, simply cut the sheet into four quadrants and fold each one following steps 1–4.

1 With the grit side downward, fold the sheet into four quadrants A, B, C and D, then open the sheet out flat.
2 Cut along one fold to the center as shown, then fold D over C.
3 Fold quadrants C and D upward over A.
4 Now fold quadrant B over C, D and A.

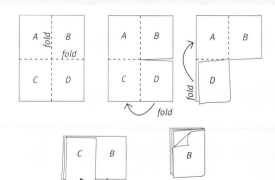

28 Sandpaper type

SANDPAPER TYPE	APPLICATIONS
Aluminum oxide	Most popular for general sanding; commonly used on wood but also for metal.
Garnet	Used for bare wood; inexpensive, but wears quickly.
Silicon carbide	Suitable for metals, plastics, fiberglass and for use between coats on paint.

29 Sandpaper rolls

Sandpaper can be purchased in the form of a roll rather than individual sheets. This is very economical if you have lots of sanding work to do. It can be cut to length and some brands have a hook and loop fastening system for easy replacement on sanders.

30 Adhesives

There are a great many adhesives available, claiming to stick just about anything to anything – however, it is very important to choose the right adhesive for the job. In other words, you can't use wallpaper paste to stick wood together, and wood glue doesn't work on plastic. In general it is best to buy specialty adhesives for glass, metal or plastic if and when you need them, as some products don't keep well once opened. For home decorating the following are always useful to have at hand:

- **PVA** Water-based, general-purpose glue for use on paper and fabric.
- **Wood glue** Designed to be stronger than the wood itself when dry. Use when joining or repairing wood.
- **Instant grab adhesive** An innovative product available in a tube that will hold things in place without the use of nails. Useful for holding wall-mounted items steady while more secure fixings are inserted.

31 Fillers

There is a multitude of fillers available for all sorts of different materials, and these can be purchased in tubes, tubs or in powder form to mix yourself – even in cartridges to be used with a gun. As with adhesives, it is best to buy specialty fillers when required as they may harden after opening. These two basic fillers will see you through most decorating jobs in the home, though, so keep a small tub or tube of each in your toolbox.

- **Decorator's filler** An all-purpose, ready-mixed filler suitable for small interior or exterior filling jobs. Most suitable for surface imperfections in plasterwork in preparation for wallpaper or paint. It is easy to use, dries white and can be sanded smooth when dry.
- **Wood filler** Designed specifically for wood, and dries hard enough to be drilled. Usually available in several shades to match the natural wood color, but a fairly light-colored filler would be most suitable for sanding down and overpainting.

32 Miscellaneous extras

- **Tapes** No decorating kit should be without a few rolls of low-tack decorator's tape for masking off areas that you don't want painted, like glass in window frames, or carpet.
- **Cloths** Always have a few cleaning cloths handy for wiping away minor spills and keeping your hands clean.
- **Cleaners** Keep a bottle of mineral spirits close by to clean hands, brushes and splatters on woodwork or windows.

Wet-and-dry

TRY IT

Rejuvenate your tape

Masking tape can deteriorate if cold or left unwrapped; before you throw it away, try this tip. Place the roll of tape together with a glass of water in the microwave oven. Cook on full power for a minute; the tape will be warm and pliable again.

Tiling tools

When decorating your home you may need to repair a broken tile, or replace tiles if you're changing a color scheme. Tiling requires a few specialized tools in addition to your basic toolbox. Most are inexpensive, with the exception of a good-quality tile-cutting jig. It is worth investing in if you have a lot of large tiles to cut – or you could hire one. Remember to use waterproof tile adhesive and grout.

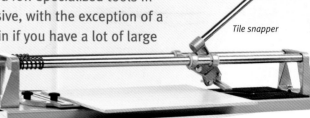

Tile snapper

33   Adhesives, grout and essential kit

Adhesives and grout are sold ready-mixed in tubes and tubs. Always use waterproof varieties for areas that are likely to be splashed with water. You will also need the following items:

- **Notched grout spreader** A hand tool that has notched blades for spreading tile adhesive in even ridges across the wall surface, to ensure uniform tile adhesion.

- **Tile spacers** Small plastic cross-shaped spacers for use with standard tiles to ensure even spacing. Some tiles have beveled edges and are self-spacing.

- **Grout refinishing kit** Most kits contain a grout rake for removing old grout, a rubber squeegee to force grout between the tiles, and a grout shaper for finishing the grout lines off smoothly.

- **Sealant and cartridge gun** A bead of silicone sealant should always be applied to the join between the tile and surface, e.g. the sink or bathtub.

- **Sponge** Use a damp sponge for wiping grout residue from tile surfaces when the job is complete.

34   Cutting and shaping

Most tiling tasks will at some stage involve encountering an obstacle that requires a tile or two to be cut or shaped – at a corner or around some pipework, for example. While cutting and shaping tiles is not a difficult task, it does require a little practice. So if you know you have some to do, make sure you have a few spare tiles to allow for mistakes and breakages. It's always handy to keep a few spares just in case a tile gets damaged in the future, too. For expert cutting and shaping you'll need the following items:

- **Chinagraph or wax pencil** For measuring and marking out; an ordinary pencil will not work on the shiny surface.

- **Tile nipper** Used for nibbling small pieces of tile to match a profile template.

- **Tile saw** Best used to cut out complicated shapes.

- **Tile file** This tool has an abrasive surface and is used to smooth off cut edges.

- **Tile scorer** This tool is used with a straight edge to score a line along a tile in readiness for cutting; most useful for small tiles.

- **Tile snapper** Used to snap a tile along a scored edge.

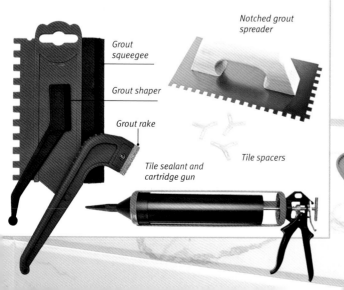

Notched grout spreader

Grout squeegee

Grout shaper

Grout rake

Tile spacers

Tile sealant and cartridge gun

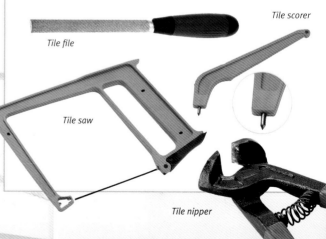

Tile file

Tile scorer

Tile saw

Tile nipper

Miscellaneous hardware

This section is all about the standard nails, screws and fixings that you may need to complete a home-decorating job – even a small task usually requires some kind of fixing or joining or a screw here and there. Each item has been designed for a specific purpose, so it's important to have a clear idea of what you need and why you need it.

35 Hammering nails

A hammer with a wooden handle has a natural spring, and so may be easier to control when nailing than one with a metal handle. It's a good idea to wear safety goggles when hammering nails into hard materials such as masonry. You may have to use quite a bit of force, potentially causing chips or grit particles to fly off.

TRY IT

The right way to knock in a nail

Hammering in a nail may seem like the simplest thing in the world to do; however, as with all things there is a right way and a wrong way to do it. Follow these simple guidelines to make sure that you don't bend the nail or flatten your fingers.

1. First blunt the nail point to reduce the chance of splitting timber. Place the head on a hard flat surface and lightly tap the tip with your hammer.

2. Hold the nail between thumb and forefinger in the correct position, then tap lightly with the hammer to engage the tip of the nail with the surface of the material.

3. To prevent the hammer missing the nail and engaging with your fingers, use long-nosed pliers. Clasp the nail shaft securely, keeping your fingers a safe distance from the hammer head.

4. If you bend the nail while hammering, you will have to remove it. The pliers will help, but using the hammer correctly will help more. Always hammer firmly but slowly, checking the nail between strikes.

5. When the nail is partially driven home you may remove the pliers (or your fingers) and finish off the job with a few firm strikes. Job done.

36 Nails you will need

Everyone knows what a nail looks like: a narrow steel fixing with a head at one end and a sharp point at the other, driven in by whacking it with a hammer. Use nails when you are joining items together that are unlikely to be dismantled. As with most DIY hardware there are lots to choose from; shown here are the most useful kinds to have at the ready.

NAIL TYPE	DESCRIPTION	APPLICATIONS
Wire nails	Oval-shaped wire nails are the most useful – 1 in, 2 in or 3 in (25 mm, 50 mm or 76 mm) in length.	General carpentry, box making. Can be driven below the surface without risk of splitting the wood.
Panel nails	Fine round nails, ⅝–2 in (15–50 mm) in length.	For use with thin panels and for fixing wooden trims to thicker pieces.
Masonry nails	Very hard round nails, 1–4 in (25–100 mm) in length.	For fixing wood to solid masonry.
Flooring nails	Rectangular tapering section; a thick shape stamped from a metal sheet.	Securing floorboards to the wooden joists underneath.

37   Types of screws

Screws are different from nails in that they have a threaded shaft that creates a strong, pull-resistant fixing, but one that can be easily removed using a screwdriver. Some screws have an entirely threaded shaft, while others have a smooth section below the head.

Screws may have slotted or cross (Pozidriv or Phillips) recesses in the head for use with corresponding screwdrivers. Screw heads may be countersunk (A), raised head (B) or raised and countersunk (C).

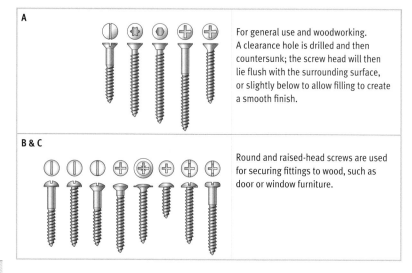

A

For general use and woodworking. A clearance hole is drilled and then countersunk; the screw head will then lie flush with the surrounding surface, or slightly below to allow filling to create a smooth finish.

B & C

Round and raised-head screws are used for securing fittings to wood, such as door or window furniture.

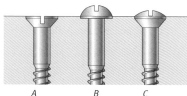

A   B   C

38   The old soft soap treatment!

Driving screws into woodwork or timber studs within a wall can require quite a lot of effort. It may be tempting to drill a larger hole, but resist! Instead, simply rub the thread of each screw along the moistened surface of a bar of soap (any soap will suffice); the soap acts as a lubricant, facilitating much easier insertion.

39   Heading in the right direction

Remember – "Righty tighty, lefty loosey." Rotate the screwdriver in a clockwise direction to insert a screw and counterclockwise to remove it. It can be easy to get confused, especially when using a power screwdriver.

FIX IT

Removing stubborn screws

There is nothing more frustrating than trying to remove a stripped screw (where the indentations in the head have been damaged so your screwdriver doesn't fit properly, preventing easy removal). If your screwdriver is slipping, stop and consider the following options to prevent further damage.

- Place a wide rubber band between the screwdriver and the screw head. When you press the screwdriver into place the rubber fills the gaps in the damaged screw head and creates a better grip so you can unscrew with ease.

- Similar to the rubber band method, use a small amount of steel wool, or the green abrasive part of a kitchen scouring pad, between screw head and screwdriver. The abrasive material will create a little more grip, so you may slowly remove the screw.

- Engage the screwdriver with the screw head and gently tap with a hammer. This may drive the blade or point of a cross-head driver into the screw head just enough to gain a little purchase. Press quite hard to remove the screw.

- If your stripped screw is a cross-head, try using a similarly sized flat-head screwdriver; there may just be enough room to push in the blade, giving enough leverage to shift the screw. You could also try the rubber band method.

- Managed to get the screw partway out and now it won't budge? Take a pair of needle-nosed pliers and clamp the jaws around the shaft of the screw. Rotate the pliers as you unscrew in order to coax the screw loose.

40 Wall fixings

You can't drive a screw directly into a wall because it will not hold securely, unless you have timber-framed walls and are drilling directly into the wood.

- **Solid masonry** You will need to drill a hole using a masonry bit, then insert a plastic screw anchor into the hole. As the screw is driven in, the sides of the anchor expand to provide extra grip. Screws and corresponding anchor sets are readily available in several standard sizes.

- **Hollow walls and ceilings** A different procedure is required here, because once the screw has penetrated the surface it will meet with a void or cavity on the other side. You need to anchor the screw on the inside of the wall. The type of fixing required depends on the load of the item to be secured (see Chapter 4, page 148 for how to use wall fixings).

ITEM TYPE	FIXING	WALL APPLICATIONS	CEILING APPLICATIONS
Lightweight item (under 10 lb/4.5 kg) *Self-drill wall screw*	• Plastic or metal self-drill screw anchors that screw into the pilot hole, ready to take the fixing screw. • The screw anchor cuts its own thread when screwed into a small starter hole. It will stay securely in the wall if the screw is removed.	• Small pictures, message boards, clocks, small/lightweight mirrors.	• Not suitable for use on ceilings.
Medium-weight item (10–25 lb/4.5–11 kg) *Plastic wall cavity fixing*	• Collapsible plastic cavity wall fixings are driven through the pilot hole. The screw is inserted and the end of the fixing is drawn back toward the inside surface, forcing two wings to project outward. The wings grip the inside surface tightly, holding the item secure.	• Small bathroom cabinets, framed pictures, medium-sized mirrors, kitchen base cabinets.	• Lightweight lighting tracks and fittings.
Heavyweight item (25–50 lb/11–22 kg) *Metal wall cavity fixing*	• Heavy-duty metal fixings also have mechanisms that grip the inner surface of the wall; some have collapsible wings while others have spring toggles. • Toggle fixings can only be used once. When the screw is removed the toggle will fall into the cavity behind the wall.	• Kitchen wall cupboards, shelving brackets, coat hooks, curtain tracks/poles, heavy framed mirrors/pictures.	• Heavy light fittings, pull-cord switches, curtain tracks/poles, decorative hanging plant holders, candle holders.

Types of paint

Paint comes in all colors of the rainbow and in varying qualities and surface finishes. It can be water-based or alkyd-based (oil/mineral-based) and varies quite a lot in price. Paint can take the form of a primer, undercoat or topcoat, and while they are not strictly called paints we can place stains and varnishes in the same category.

TRY IT

Tinted primer
Professional decorators often add a color tint that matches the topcoat to white primer. Tints for alkyd and latex paints are available at the paint store – be sure to ask when you buy your paint.

41 Priming basics

In general if the surface you want to paint is bare – wood, metal, plaster, drywall – then you will need to apply a suitable primer first in order for subsequent paint layers to adhere properly. A quality product will produce a better finished result. Primer is designed to bond with a bare surface to create a durable base that prevents the paint layer from peeling or cracking. In addition, using a primer before painting often reduces the number of coats required to achieve adequate coverage. Different primers are formulated for use with different surfaces as a base for paint or as a sealant for porous surfaces such as concrete or brick. Make sure to choose the correct primer for the job.

PRIMER TYPE	APPLICATIONS	NOTES
Oil-based	Use with oil-based paint. Good for preventing bleed-through from unfinished wood.	Require mineral spirits for thinning and cleaning up. High odor.
Latex	As a base for latex/water-based paints, and for interior and exterior surfaces including woodwork, drywall, plaster, masonry, brick and painted metal.	Low odor and easy clean.
All-purpose	Useful general-purpose primer for interior and exterior applications; versatile with strong adhesive properties.	Low odor and easy clean.
Enamel	Usually applied to bare metal and wooden surfaces; serves both as a protective and decorative coat.	Available in various finishes and can be sanded prior to painting to achieve a smooth surface.
All-in-one paint/ primer	A combined paint and primer product, providing a good seal and coverage in one coat. Ideal for use on previously painted surfaces.	Pay attention to your budget; work out before purchase if it is cheaper to buy primer and paint or a combined product.

42 Latex or alkyd?

Which to choose? Before you make your paint purchase you may like to evaluate the pros and cons of a water-based latex versus an oil-based alkyd product.

LATEX	ALKYD
• Water-based; not harmful to the environment.	• Clean with thinner or solvent.
• Clean with water.	• 12 hours' minimum drying time.
• Quick drying.	• Can have a strong odor.
• Low odor.	• Usually (but not always) a high-gloss finish.
• Range of surface finishes.	• High durability; best suited to woodwork, doors or window trim.
• Durable; suitable for most interior paint jobs.	• Suitable for use in low temperatures.
• Shows brush marks if used in very low temperatures.	• Can be sensitive to light; some fading can occur through UV exposure.
• Good sheen and color retention; good adherence.	

Latex matte paint has been used to create flat wall coverage. A gloss-finish, alkyd-based paint has been used on the stairway.

TRY IT

Testing, testing!

Buy a tester pot of paint before investing in a whole room's worth; paint is expensive and mistakes can be costly. When you get home, don't paint a test patch on the wall right away; instead paint a few sheets of white letter-size paper and pin them up in different positions in the room, next to your curtains or sofa, for instance. Differences in light and proximity to other colors can make a big difference to how the paint looks.

43 Specialty paint options

You might like to try the following specialty paints:

- **Metallic paint** Perfect for feature walls, furniture and special effects.

- **Blackboard paint** Good old-fashioned matte black stuff you can chalk on. Good for making message boards in kitchens, offices or children's rooms.

- **Magnetic paint** A fun element to think of when planning your decor; useful for studies, offices, kitchens or just for fun. Use pretty magnets to hold your notes.

- **Light-reflecting paint** These paints have special light-reflecting particles and are best used in low-light areas, hallways or rooms with small windows and little natural light. These paints can really make a difference, not only to light but to perceived space.

- **Floor paint** Hardwearing paint product designed for use on wood, concrete and even vinyl flooring.

- **Makeover paint** Designed specifically for home decor revamps such as kitchen cabinets; high durability.

A trompe l'oeil striped carpet runner effect is applied to a wooden staircase using colorful, hardwearing floor paints. Neat stripes are created simply by masking off each strip in turn using low-tack decorator's tape. A steady hand will make this easier to achieve!

Wallpaper

Wallpaper has two advantages over paint finishes: it can cover walls and ceilings with a regular pattern or design, and it can provide a surface texture. The finished effect may be purely decorative, or it can offer practical benefits too – for example, it may be hardwearing and easy to clean. Wallpaper hanging can seem like an awkward task, but once you have mastered the basic techniques it is a relatively quick decorating option.

TRY IT

Easy pasting

If you are an inexperienced home decorator, try using ready-pasted wallpaper. The rolls have a layer of paste on the reverse side, and all you'll need is a special water trough in which to soak the rolls. Simply immerse the roll in the trough, then unroll and apply directly to the wall.

44 Working with flocked paper

Highly textured flocked wallpapers or hand-blocked designs can be expensive and are generally sold in smaller rolls – that is, you'll get fewer feet (meters) per roll to play with than regular wallpaper. Make sure to calculate carefully before you buy. You'll also have to be careful when pasting and hanging this type of paper as the paste can stain and spoil delicate surface textures.

45 Using vintage papers

It can be tempting to buy vintage wallpapers, but buyer beware! Rolls of wallpaper that are a few decades old may be faded or worn at the edges, which can make matching difficult for a large wall. However, they do make a fabulous feature, and if you can use small sections somewhere in your new decor then go for it.

46 Making the most of wallpaper

- **Floral wallpaper** Floral wallpaper has a rustic and old-fashioned charm, which is completely in keeping with traditional styles. When restoring an old house, floral wallpapers will help create an authentic appearance.

- **Borders and friezes** Usually hung at chair or picture-rail level, but can be used elsewhere, for example around base boards or as a fun feature in children's rooms.

- **High-traffic areas** Hallways can benefit from durable, washable, scrubbable vinyl-coated wallcoverings.

- **Narrow areas** These are usually better suited to plain wallpapers, perhaps with small patterns. Large bold designs can be tiring on the eyes and make the place look smaller and more cluttered. You can also limit the use of paper to below a chair rail if you want the best of both worlds.

- **Disguising faults** Good-quality wallpaper can cover a multitude of cracks and blemishes in poorly finished walls and ceilings, making it an invaluable resource for decorating older houses.

- **Design variety** You name it, and you can find a wallpaper that features it! Stripes, spots, novelty prints, oversized abstract designs, reproduction vintage style.

- **Illusion** You can use wallpaper to create the illusion of space. Stripes can give a feeling of height and spaciousness in a small room.

- **Hand-printed wallpapers** These are specialty papers that are expensive and not widely available. They are suitable for feature walls, accents and period themes.

- **Metallic finishes** These are not easy to apply, but they can create spectacular effects in the modern home.

47 Wallpaper options

- Woodchip
- Vinyl-coated paper
- Embossed paper
- Textured paper
- Flocked wallpaper
- Hand-printed wallpaper
- Specialty papers
- Textile wallcovering
- Patterned papers

1. Stripes don't have to be bold! Using subtle pastel shades can add light and texture to large, plain wall areas. Crisp white paint and flooring tiles, combined with pale wood fixtures, create a fresh, contemporary feel, especially in halls and entrance ways.

2. Small bedroom spaces with low or sloping ceilings can sometimes be overwhelmed by large patterns. However, ornate furniture and delicate color combinations can detract from the scale of the wallpaper pattern, giving an impression of coziness and femininity.

3. Light plays an important part in any decorating scheme, whether your light source is natural or from carefully placed lighting fixtures. Patterned wallpapers or those with reflective pattern or texture can add surface interest without adding strong color.

4. Very dark colors make a dramatic statement when used as a feature wall, but can make a room look gloomy. Lighten the mood by using a geometric, textured paper instead of flat color. Matching furniture looks sleek and modern while pale flooring adds light and space.

5. Op art meets the Arts and Crafts movement! Characteristic decorative elements from different styles can be used in your decorating scheme both to contrast and complement. One delicate shade is picked out from the patterned throw pillow and reflected in the wall color.

2

4

5

PAINT KNOW-HOW

How to choose paint

48 Paint is probably the product most frequently used by home decorators, and it is readily available. DIY stores are brimming with all kinds of paints designed specifically for use with different surface materials. Here you'll find out how to make informed purchasing choices based on more than just color and cost per can, and how to prepare and look after your paint when you get it home.

WHAT IS PAINT?

Paint is a mixture of very finely ground solid particles of pigment that are suspended in a water-based, or oil-/mineral-based liquid. When the liquid is applied to a surface it dries to form a decorative and protective layer. Resins or binding agents are used to ensure the pigment particles adhere soundly to the surface to be painted. Inexpensive paint has a higher percentage of solvent to volume and so contains less pigment and resin than a higher-quality product. After application, the water or solvent evaporates and the paint is seen to dry, leaving behind the colored pigment on the surface – it follows then that less pigment results in a poorer coverage and color intensity.

50

TIPS FOR CHOOSING QUALITY PAINT

49

Paint prices are a pretty accurate reflection of quality. As a general rule try to buy the best paint that your budget will allow. Higher-quality paints are easier to use, give better coverage, require fewer coats and offer greater durability than cheaper alternatives, so are better value for money in the long run.

✳ **Color** Think of your home as a whole; try to choose colors that will complement each other or existing schemes. Good-quality paints are usually available in a wider range of colors and finishes than cheaper alternatives.

✳ **Durability** Traffic and humidity are two important things to bear in mind when choosing paint. Choose scrubbable, scuff-resistant or waterproof paints for areas that are likely to receive rough treatment, such as hallways, childrens' rooms or kitchens and bathrooms. The pigments contained in bargain paint may "chalk" and be washed or worn away with repeated rubbing or scrubbing.

✳ **Coverage** Apply one or two coats of acrylic paint in order to mask previous colors. Remember, if multiple coats are required consider a water-based product, as the drying time will be faster. Coverage will be listed on the can label, and on average is about 400 sq. ft (37 sq. m) per gallon. Bargain paints may require two or even three coats to cover the same area as one coat of better-quality paint.

Touch-up tip

51

If you have a small amount of leftover paint in a large can, decant it into a clean plastic water bottle. Now drop a glass marble into the bottle and replace the screw top. Label the bottle clearly with the paint color, make and manufacturer's code and finish, and which room you used it in for your information. When you need to touch up scuffs or marks, simply shake the bottle, and the marble will mix the paint ready for application.

TWO STEPS TO PREPARE PAINT

• **Stirring** Paint contains solid particles that can sometimes sink to the bottom of the can. Use a clean, flat batten or stirring stick to stir the paint to a uniform consistency. Note that some paints are non-stir.

• **Straining** Old paint can be reused, but may contain bits of dried paint or other debris from the previous job. These will spoil your paint finish, so strain the paint through a pair of nylon pantyhose into a clean container.

52

53 Top tips for storing paint

* Sunlight can be bad for paint. Always store it in a dark place away from direct sunlight.

* Excessive heat, cold or humidity can also damage paint. Avoid storage areas at risk from frost, dampness or overheating.

* Paint can be stored for up to five years quite safely, though small quantities keep better if decanted into smaller containers.

* If old paint appears to have "separated" in the can, simply stir well, and if the paint mixes to a sound consistency then it will be good to use.

* When storing a half-used can of paint, make sure the lid is on firmly, then turn it upside down. That way, if a skin forms on the surface it will be on the bottom of the can when you turn it the right way up and open it for use.

* Always clean the lid and the rim of the can before closing to store it. Paint buildup can create an inadequate seal that will allow air into the can, spoiling the paint.

* Cover the top of the can with a layer of plastic food wrap before replacing the lid; this will protect against air contamination.

* To avoid damaging the lid, place a wooden batten across the lid and then tap it home using a hammer. A rubber mallet works well too.

* Remember to label the cans clearly for future use.

✳ ✳ ✳ ✳ ✳ ✳ ✳ ✳ ✳ ✳ ✳ ✳ ✳ ✳ ✳ ✳

PAINT SAFETY TIPS

55

* Always read the information label before using paint. The directions for use will indicate drying times, clean-up procedures and what to do if paint comes into contact with skin or eyes, as paint may contain chemicals that are poisonous, flammable or irritant. Take heed of any warnings and instructions for safe handling.

* Pour paint thinner/cleaner into a clear jar after use. When the solid material from brushes has settled to the bottom, pour off the clean thinner and save for reuse later. Dispose of the sediment as hazardous waste.

* Make sure cans of paint and paint products are kept safely out of reach of children and animals.

✳ ✳ ✳ ✳ ✳ ✳ ✳ ✳ ✳ ✳ ✳ ✳ ✳ ✳ ✳ ✳ ✳ ✳

54 OPENING AND CLOSING THE CAN

* Never use a chisel to pry off a paint can lid. You may damage the blade and the rim of the lid.

* Some paint manufacturers provide a handy tool specially designed for popping off lids. Keep it handy in your toolbox.

* Brush any dust or dirt from the top of the can; it will contaminate the paint if allowed to drop inside.

* You can use a large flat-bladed screwdriver to open a can. Place the tip of the screwdriver under the lid's rim at an angle of about 35–40 degrees. Now, gently lower the screwdriver a few degrees, then move it a little way around the rim and repeat. The idea is to gently loosen the lid without causing damage.

* Air is the enemy of paint. Lids are designed to fit tightly, so it pays to keep the lid clean. Wipe off excess paint then store the lid in a plastic bag when not in use so the paint doesn't cake around the edge.

56 Opening old paint cans

Old rusty paint can? Stuck lid? Gnarled and damaged rim due to a clumsy opening procedure last time? Excessive and forceful levering with a screwdriver will cause further damage to the rim, leaving you without any rim on which to use your lever. Grab your pliers and follow these simple steps:

1. Grip the rim in the jaws of the pliers, holding them at a shallow angle to the lid, then gently lever the pliers downward.

2. Release the jaws and move a little way around the can and repeat.

3. This action will help to flatten out the damaged rim and gently ease out the lid.

4. Work slowly and patiently, and eventually the lid will free itself.

5. It's a good idea to decant the paint into another receptacle for storage, as you won't be able to reuse the old can successfully.

9 Nifty gadgets

Here's a selection of non-essential but really useful stuff that you may want to consider adding to your toolbox. As ever, if you don't need it, don't buy it – especially if storage space is at a premium – however, some things are so useful it's worth having them just in case.

1 Workbench

A small portable workbench that is easy to carry around and folds flat for storage can be invaluable for lots of home-decorating tasks. You can take it with you to the work area for use as a steady platform for sawing, drilling and general assembly or marking out. The top can be used as a vise, and has several adjustable devices for holding things steady while you work.

2 Laser level

If you have a nice long spirit level then you don't really need this, but it is a really good way of plotting long straight lines on vertical or horizontal planes. It's also useful for marking guidelines when putting up battens for shelves, or hanging wallpaper.

3 Stud finder (or cable/pipe detector)

This is most useful when you want to drill into walls safely. It is a battery-powered handheld device that detects the presence of unseen cables and pipes, or timber framework (studs) behind drywall. The advantages are that you won't drill into cables or pipes by mistake and/or will find a suitable stud in which to make a secure fixing.

4 Sliding bevel

This is a very neat little tool with a folding adjustable blade. Use it to measure internal angles, then use the tool to mark off your cutting lines. It's handy when cutting shelves to fit alcoves that aren't straight (see page 152 for more on cutting shelves).

5 C-clamps

A set of three differently sized C-clamps can come in very handy if you need to hold something steady while you glue, saw, drill or screw. They're called C-clamps because they look like the letter "C" in profile.

6 Miter saw

This is a really easy device to use for making neat straight and angled cuts in timber and wooden moldings. It's useful when cutting cornices, chair or picture rails to size, or if you fancy a spot of picture framing. You can set the saw to cut any angle you like.

7 Crowbars

A couple of small crowbars or pry bars can really make light work of lifting floorboards, prying off paneling or base boards, or removing large stubborn nails. The length of the bar adds a little valuable leverage, and makes the job easier.

8 Rubber mallet

This is just like a hammer, but with a rubber head instead of a metal one. It is really useful when assembling flatpack furniture: you can safely whack dowel-jointed sections together without damaging the surface.

9 Gripping pliers

These are similar to regular pliers, but they can also be used as a clamp. The jaws can be adjusted to size and then locked to grip items firmly while you work. They're invaluable if you're on your own and need an extra hand.

2 Planning and preparation

Any home decorating project will soon founder without a well-thought-out plan of action and a sound knowledge of the processes required. Home decoration can be a most rewarding experience but good planning and thorough preparation are the keys to a successful outcome. This chapter will help you to formulate a plan and set achievable goals, make good colour and style choices, estimate types and quantities of material, and then learn the preparation techniques required for the task ahead. Be ambitious but know your limitations; be prepared to learn new skills, and remember — practice makes perfect!

Order of work

Once you have decided what you need to do, you will need to make a clear and comprehensive order of work. A clear plan of action will help your time management, ensure you have the right tools, equipment and materials required, and will ultimately ensure the work runs smoothly. There is no straightforward answer to how much time and effort will be required to redecorate a room; a lot depends on the condition of the room, your skill and experience and the amount of free time you have.

TRY IT

Make a list

Get yourself a notebook, jot down everything you need to do and rearrange it on a page in whatever way suits you: a mind map, a chart, a bulleted list. You could start with a list and then take a new page for each room, adding notes as you go. Use the checklists, charts and tips that follow as a guide.

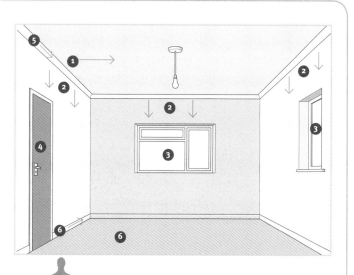

FIX IT

Watch your step

Cover walk-through areas with drop cloths; you don't want to tread paint right through the house on your shoes. However, if you do, try the following:

- **For water-based latex paint** Flush area with cold water, then sponge away the paint with warm soapy water. Blot dry with a clean cloth.
- **Alkyd/oil-based paint** Apply paint cleaner (as suggested on the paint can) or mineral spirits to the area, then blot.

57   Where to start first?

1. Start with the ceiling and work down. Always begin at the door and work away from it. If you are painting, any splashes that fall on the walls can easily be painted or papered over.

2. Walls are the next large area to be decorated; again, work from top to bottom and away from the doorway.

3. Window frames and windowsills are next. (See Chapter 4, page 131 for how to paint different styles of windows in a logical sequence.)

4. Doors and door frames are next. (See Chapter 4, page 128 for a foolproof painting system.)

5. Paint cornices when both ceiling and walls are dry.

6. The final stage is the base board and floor area. Always apply floor treatments or coverings last.

58   Practical considerations

- It's better to decorate in summertime; warmer weather = more hours of daylight.
- In warm weather you can open windows for ventilation.
- Cold weather can affect drying times and paint finishes.
- Time management – Try to plan a continuous work session in order to minimize disruption to the household.

59   From top to bottom

It makes sense to work from the top down when decorating a room – but this also works when decorating a whole house. Remember, dust and dirt will gravitate downward, so start with the upstairs rooms first. If you're working on just one room, make sure the doors to other rooms are closed to prevent dust migration.

60 Checklist: 20 things to think about

1. Are there any major structural alterations to be carried out before decorating? Consider these first. ☐

2. Do you need to employ a professional to install power sockets, move radiators, relocate wiring or pipes, etc? These jobs should be carried out prior to decorating. ☐

3. Tools and equipment check – Make a list, check it twice. Have you got everything you need? ☐

4. Materials – Measure up and make quantity estimations. Purchase what you require. ☐

5. Diary check – Always allow plenty of time to complete the task, and to clean up afterward. Mistakes are made in haste. Mark in your decorating days. ☐

6. Move all furniture from the work area if possible. ☐

7. Consider where you will put furniture to cause minimum clutter and inconvenience. ☐

8. Unscrew and remove any fixtures if possible: curtain tracks, shelf brackets and so on. Remember to keep the screws safe. ☐

9. Remove old floorcoverings, strip wallpaper and strip paint job if necessary. ☐

10. Prepare and make good all surfaces to be decorated: walls, ceilings, woodwork. ☐

11. Clean, wash and rub down walls and ceilings, woodwork and trims. ☐

12. Vacuum or sweep floors, and remove dust and debris before wallpapering or painting. ☐

13. Mask off or cover anything you don't want painted. Use plenty of drop cloths for the floor and to cover furniture that has been left in situ. ☐

14. Check the order of work for decorating, and proceed in a logical fashion. ☐

15. Replace fixtures.

16. Carry out a final sweep to remove decorating debris, and check flooring is sound – for example, fix loose boards. ☐

17. Install new flooring. ☐

18. Reinstate furniture. This is a good opportunity to rearrange it, too. ☐

19. Replace or reinstall soft furnishings, curtains, blinds, etc. ☐

20. Tools and equipment check – Clean tools and reinstate in toolbox. Store equipment, paint and other materials appropriately. Job done. ☐

61 Assessing the situation

First make sure that you know what you're dealing with – you really don't want any surprises when you lift a carpet or peel away the wallpaper, only to find damp, rot or worse. Inspect your project site thoroughly, then deal with big issues and structural alterations. Unexpected extra work can delay your decorating process; a quick decorating job can turn into a marathon if most of your plasterwork comes off with the old wallpaper or if the fireplace surround or floorboards require more attention than you had planned. Calculate for the worst, then you won't be frustrated by unexpected delays.

ABOVE: After stripping off wallpaper there may be lots of surface repair and preparation to do.

LEFT: Floorboards in poor condition must be repaired before sanding or using floorcoverings.

Mold and mildew caused by damp.

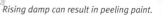

Rising damp can result in peeling paint.

FIX IT

When to call in the professionals?

It is essential to get certain big issues fixed before decorating – and it may well be time to call in the professionals.

BIG ISSUE	SYMPTOMS	CAUSE	FIX
Rising damp	Tidemark on walls indicates the level to which moisture has risen.	Damage to damp-proof membrane (DPM) situated about 12 in (30 cm) above ground level.	Re-lay DPM or apply DPM liquid.
Penetrating damp	Wet or damp patches on walls or ceilings.	Water leaking through walls, most often caused by structural damage such as faulty guttering or roofing.	Correct structural faults. Apply damp-proof paint to mask damp stains.
Infestations			
Woodworm	Appearance of small exit holes in wood.	Insects	Application of insecticide.
Dry rot	Wood becomes cracked; appearance of mushroom-like growths on surface and musty smell.	Fungus	Remove and replace affected wood; treat with specialty product.
Wet rot	Wood becomes dark, soft and pulpy.	Fungus	Remove and replace affected wood; treat with specialty product.
Subsidence	Wide cracks in the walls, especially near windows and doors.	Ground under house drying out due to drought or proximity to large trees.	Foundations must be underpinned for support.
Condensation	Damp patches on walls, ceilings, black mold, misting windows.	When warm, moist air meets a cold surface.	Introduce adequate ventilation or insulation.

Wet rot

Woodworm

Dry rot

Surface considerations: walls, ceilings and floors

Before you begin a decorating project it's worth spending some time examining your walls, ceilings and floors. What they're made of and their construction can influence how you proceed with the job and will also indicate the tools and skills you may need for repair and renovation – it can also limit your choices. The walls, ceilings and floors are structural elements of your home, but from the decorator's point of view they are also nice large planes offering great scope for creativity.

62   Know your walls

Unless you're decorating or hanging a picture, you may not think much about walls. But the walls in your home offer structure, security, privacy, sound insulation, protection from fire – oh yes, and you can decorate them too! Walls may be solid or constructed with a cavity between the surfaces.

	SOLID MASONRY	MADE FROM SOLID BRICK
External walls	Cavity	Two brick walls separated by a cavity that can be filled with insulating material.
	Timber-framed	Timber-framed houses can have a solid outer wall and a drywall layer inside.
Internal walls	Brick or block	Interior load-bearing walls may be solid brick or block construction, skimmed with a plaster layer.
	Lath and plaster	Non-load-bearing walls may be timber-framed with a lath and plaster covering.
	Drywall	Non-load-bearing walls or partition walls can be timber frames covered with drywall panels.

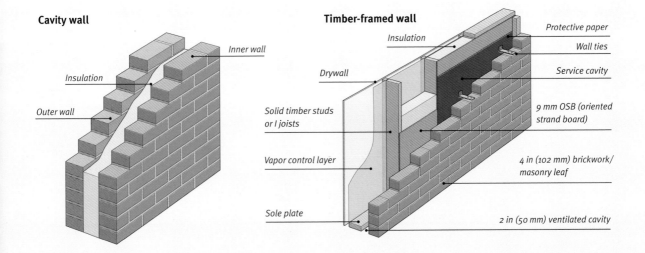

Cavity wall

Inner wall

Insulation

Outer wall

Timber-framed wall

Insulation

Drywall

Solid timber studs or I joists

Vapor control layer

Sole plate

Protective paper

Wall ties

Service cavity

9 mm OSB (oriented strand board)

4 in (102 mm) brickwork/ masonry leaf

2 in (50 mm) ventilated cavity

63   Plaster and drywall characteristics

Interior walls are most commonly constructed from plaster or drywall. Wallpaper, paint finishes and tiles can be applied to sound, smooth wall surfaces regardless of what they're made of. Just remember that preparation pays – all surfaces must be adequately prepared before you apply a decorative treatment.

PLASTER	DRYWALL
A wall construction technique found in older homes; involves the application of plaster to a solid wall, which creates a smooth, hard surface when dried. • Durable finish. • Screw anchors must be used when making secure fixings.	Drywall panels are secured to timber-framed walls using nails and tape. • Less durable than plaster. • Can be coated with veneer plaster to give the appearance of plaster. • Special drywall or cavity wall fixings must be used when installing fixtures.

64   Six need-to-know facts about drywall

- The term "drywall" refers to the fact that drywall panels are installed dry, unlike plaster, which uses water and is applied to the wall wet.

- Drywall panels are made from gypsum, which is a word derived from the Latin term "gypsos" (plaster). Drywall is a layer of gypsum sandwiched between two layers of lining paper.

- As a home-decoration material, drywall has an advantage over plaster in that there are no lengthy drying times involved.

- Drywall has good sound insulation properties and can reduce noise transmission. High-performance drywall has a specially made core that provides an even better barrier against sound.

- You can easily apply wallpaper directly onto the paper surface of the drywall panel, but it is better practice to seal the paper surface of the drywall using a drywall sealer. This will also facilitate easier wallpaper stripping later.

- Cracks in the taped joins between drywall panels are usually caused by the warping of the wall's internal timber framework or general settlement of the building. Screw fixings are less likely to cause cracking than nail fixings.

Lath and plaster construction found in older properties

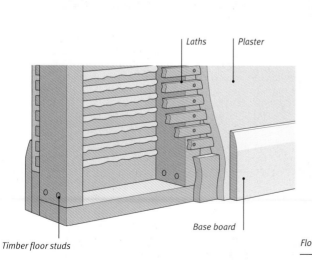

Laths

Plaster

Base board

Timber floor studs

Drywall panels and timber or metal framework construction

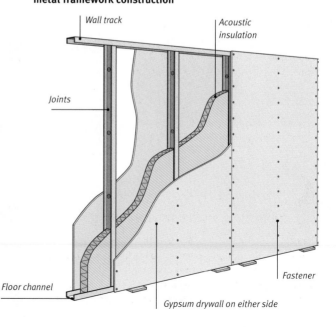

Wall track

Acoustic insulation

Joints

Floor channel

Gypsum drywall on either side

Fastener

FIX IT

Filling holes and cracks

- **Plaster** Surface blemishes may be repaired with filler. Deeper holes may be filled but will require a working-up process, and the application of layers of filling compound. Allow adequate drying time between layers.

- **Drywall** Small holes and cracks may be filled, but larger holes opening onto the cavity will require additional backing to seal the hole from the inside, then a filling layer applied on top.

TRY IT

Knock, knock!

How do you know if your walls are solid or not? Simply knock on the surface, and if it sounds hollow then it is. A dull thud indicates a solid construction.

65 Suitable applications for ceilings and floors

One major difference between floors and ceilings is that floors receive a real battering, while ceilings suffer very little wear and tear. This means that any decorative treatment needs to be fit for the job.

- **Ceilings** May be painted or wallpapered in same way as walls; high durability is not required. Many decorative treatments may be considered.

- **Floors** High durability is essential. Use carpet, tile, vinyl or laminate floorcovering or specially formulated floor paint or varnish for floorboards.

66 What you might find underfoot

Exactly what type of floor you have remains a mystery until you remove the old coverings. Solid floors and timber constructions have different properties and require appropriate methods of preparation before exploring decorative options.

FLOOR TYPE	PREPARATION	DECORATIVE TREATMENT
Concrete Your floor may just be a solid slab of concrete.	• Concrete may be dusty, crumbling and unstable. • Hollows must be filled with cement mortar and surface sealed with building adhesive.	• May be painted, or laid with ceramic or vinyl tiles, sheet vinyl flooring or carpet with suitable underlay.
Timber Wooden floorboards are suspended on and secured to wooden beams called floor joists that run across the building.	• Floorboards may be creaky, wobbly, damaged or missing. • Boards must be repaired or replaced before applying decorative treatment.	• Can be sanded and painted or stained. • Must be overlaid with hardboard sheet to create a flat, gap-free surface if laying other flooring materials such as carpet or vinyl tiles.

67 Safety – avoiding services

The gaps between the joists underneath a timber floor at ground level and between ceilings and the floor above usually house electrical wiring and pipework for water and gas. It is essential that you know where these services are when driving in nails or screws in order to prevent accidental engagement with a cable or pipe.

68 Gauging plaster thickness

Plaster can vary in thickness, which will dictate the length of screw anchors and screws you might use to attach wall fixings. Push the point of your bradawl into the plaster until you feel the resistance of the solid wall underneath. Pull the bradawl out again to judge the thickness of the plaster.

Estimating quantities

Before you begin to apply paint, paper or tiles to any surface in your home you must estimate the quantities you'll need. Different materials require different calculation methods. For example, paint is measured in gallons; wallpaper will be calculated as a number of rolls; and tiles as the total number of complete tiles to cover the area, bearing in mind that tiles are different sizes. However, the area of a wall, ceiling or tiled area is usually where you start; to work this out simply multiply the height and width together to find the area's square footage.

69 How to estimate paint quantities

This simple formula will help you calculate how much paint you will require for a single coat of your chosen space.

1. Length of wall or ceiling x height of wall, or width of ceiling = surface area

2. Surface area divided by coverage per gallon of chosen paint = gallons of paint needed

70 Estimating lining paper quantities

It is sometimes necessary to apply lining paper to walls before hanging decorative wallpaper. Lining paper is hung in horizontal bands, so the calculation method is a little different from wallpaper. Begin by calculating the area of each plane as before. Then use the table as a guide to the number of rolls you'll need.
A standard roll of lining paper is 22 in x 11 yd = 6 sq. yd (56 cm x 10 m = 5 sq. m).

Total area (sq. ft)	Total area (sq. m)	No of rolls required
6	5	1
12	10	2
18	15	3

For every additional 6 sq. yd (5 sq. m), add another roll of lining paper.

71 Working with patterned papers

If a wallpaper has a pattern then the total useable area of the roll is decreased due to the wastage involved in pattern matching.

Pattern size/drop	Useable area of roll
0–6 in (0–15 cm)	25 sq. ft (2.3 sq. m)
7–12 in (18–30 cm)	22 sq. ft (2 sq. m)
13–18 in (33–46 cm)	20 sq. ft (1.8 sq. m)
19–23 in (48– 59 cm)	only half a single roll

72 Estimating wallpaper quantities

- **Walls** Measure the perimeter of the room; ignore the doors and windows unless they comprise more than 10 percent of the perimeter. A standard roll of wallpaper is just over 20 in (51 cm) wide.

- **Ceilings** Measure the length of one strip and count how many strips you need. Calculate how many strips you can cut from a 33 ft (10 m) roll to work out how many rolls you'll need.

Note: This chart does not allow for pattern matching. In general you'll need to allow one complete pattern match extra per drop. You'll find the size of the pattern repeat on the roll label.

Wall height	Measurements around the room											
Feet	30	33	36	39	43	46	49	52	56	59	62	66
Meters	9	10	11	12	13	14	15	16	17	18	19	20
6 ft 6½ in to 7 ft 2 in (2.0 m to 2.2 m)	4	4	5	5	5	6	6	6	6	7	7	8
7 ft 2 in to 7 ft 10½ in (2.2 m to 2.4 m)	4	4	5	5	6	6	6	7	7	8	8	9
7 ft 10½ in to 8 ft 6 in (2.4 m to 2.6 m)	4	5	5	6	6	7	7	8	8	9	9	10
8 ft 6 in to 9 ft 2 in (2.6 m to 2.8 m)	5	5	6	6	7	7	8	8	9	9	10	11
9 ft 2 in to 9 ft 10 in (2.8 m to 3.0 m)	5	5	6	7	7	8	8	9	9	10	11	12

73 Estimating tile quantities

To begin, you will need to decide where your tiles are going to go, and measure the height and width of each plane carefully.

- **Method 1** Measure the tile and work out how many tiles will fit into the height and width. Multiply these figures together to estimate how many tiles you'll need for the whole job.

- **Method 2** Most packs of tiles will indicate the area each pack will cover in square feet (or square meters); simply calculate the area to be tiled and divide by the figure on the pack to calculate the number of packs you'll need.

- Count cut pieces as whole tiles in your calculation, then allow 10 percent extra for breakages.

Note: Don't forget tile adhesive and grout. The pack will indicate the wall area they will cover; simply divide the area by this figure for a rough estimate of how much you'll need.

74 Spares for repairs

If you have a spare roll of wallpaper when the job is done it is worth hanging onto it in case you need to make a repair later. Store the roll in a long cardboard mailing tube; this will keep the roll clean and prevent damage to the edges.

TRY IT

Math made easy

Now, this is not cheating – if the thought of doing the math yourself is just too much, look online. Lots of decorating product companies have automatically calculated estimation guides. Simply type in the details, press "calculate," then make your purchase. Easy.

75 Quantities for covering dark colors

Remember that if you are painting over a dark color then you will probably need to apply at least two or maybe three or more coats. Don't forget to build this into your calculation.

76 What to do with surplus tiles?

Even careful calculation could lead you to have some leftover tiles. Don't get rid of them; keep any remaining tiles safe because you may need them for repairs at a later date.

Paint or paper?

Deciding whether to use paint or paper for your decorating project largely depends on what your walls and ceiling are like in the first place and whether you already have wallpaper or paint. As with all things there are pros and cons to consider before making any purchases; paint and paper can be expensive, so it is wise to be sure before you buy. It's worth checking the DIY store's returns policy, just in case you change your mind.

TRY IT

Clever combinations

Why not try a combination of patterned and plain? Choose a bold, patterned wallpaper for a chimney breast or feature wall, then use a plain paint finish for the remaining walls. You can use a shade that blends or tones with your feature pattern, or pick up a contrasting detail color to really make a statement.

77   Factors to consider

- **Cost** Use the quantity estimators given on page 48 to make rough estimates of paint and paper requirements for each room. Do the calculations and let your budget decide for you.

- **Preparation** How much time have you got? If you have poor wall surfaces, adequate preparation for a good flat paint finish can take a long time. It may save you time to use wallpaper.

- **Ease of application** Which do you prefer? If you really hate wallpapering then perhaps paint is the answer. On the other hand, wallpapering is a quick way of adding impact and pattern.

- **Versatility** What is your room to be used for? Consider your family's lifestyle. Check durability and care instructions for paper and paint.

- **Effect** Do you want to make a bold statement with oversized patterns, or create a minimalist, understated environment with flat color?

	PAINT	PAPER
Preparation	Pros: • Ideal option when flat surface color is preferred. Cons: • Preparation of damaged walls takes a long time; allow 24 hours for filling compound to dry before painting. • Applying light paint over a dark color will require many coats. Use a tinted primer to block out the base color; it will save time.	Pros: • Good-quality wallpaper can cover up a multitude of surface sins. Choose this option if your walls are very uneven and blemished. • Provides pattern and texture. Cons: • Preparation of damaged walls takes a long time; allow 24 hours for filling compound to dry before papering. • Stripping wallpaper is a lengthy, messy job. You'll need the right tools to do it properly. • Care must be taken not to cause more damage to the walls when struggling to remove stubborn or multilayered paper.
Application	Pros: • Easy to apply with a brush, roller or paint pad. • Easy clean-up for water-based paint. • Paint is an ideal option if low cost and ease of application are priorities. Cons: • Alkyd paints have an unpleasant odor and require specialty mineral or solvent cleaners.	Pros: • Relatively swift room transformations can be achieved with the use of patterned paper. Cons: • Application techniques can be tricky to master. Straight walls are an easy task, but if your room has many awkward corners and obstacles then it will take longer.
Durability	Pros: • High-gloss/sheen paints are generally quite durable; some finishes are designed to withstand washing and scrubbing and are suitable for kitchens and bathrooms and high-traffic areas. Cons: • Plaster or drywall that has been overpainted may be prone to damage from general wear and tear. Chips, dents and scratches must be repaired and then repainted. • Flat matte paints are less durable than higher-sheen or gloss finishes.	Pros: • Some papers are highly durable and can withstand washing, scrubbing, tough treatment from children, furniture and general traffic. Check manufacturer's guidelines. Cons: • In general, rooms where high levels of moisture or steam may occur are unsuitable for wallpaper. The adhesive paste may become damp and cause the paper to peel. • Wallpaper can be ripped or torn and may require repair. • Highly embossed paper can develop flat spots. • Some high-quality specialty papers cannot be cleaned.
Variety	Pros: • Paint is available in a vast array of colors, and various finishes from flat matte to ultra glossy. • Specialty paints provide a means of decorating and protecting all sorts of surfaces in the home – walls, ceilings, woodwork, metal, plastic and ceramic.	Pros: • Wallpaper comes in a variety of colors, patterns, textures and weights. • Surface finishes can be paper- or vinyl-coated for extra durability.

1. Open-plan living areas can be linked by using the same color palette throughout. Variation in color intensity and use of pattern is a clever way of separating areas that are used in different ways. Here the office and dining areas are separated from each other by plain walls, but remain linked by a wallpaper pattern that is a combination of both colors.

2. This striped paint effect pulls the room together by incorporating the door into the scheme. The wall appears to be seamless, making the room feel larger.

3. This modern interior has a hint of Art Deco style, but is softened with innovative use of pale floral paper. The paper is cleverly used here inside a wooden frame, painted to match the paneling along the lower wall area.

4. A lovely monochromatic, traditional floral print is given a modern twist by using a strong background shade. This provides an ideal opportunity to make use of plain furniture and have fun with bright accent colors.

Surface preparation: walls

In a perfect world all our walls would be smooth and unblemished, but in reality it's never that easy. Removal of wallpaper always reveals a few imperfections, and even if you're simply freshening up old paint, it's good practice to examine the surfaces carefully and fix any holes or cracks that have occurred through normal wear and tear. There is no doubt that preparation pays; time spent on repairs is never wasted.

79　How to fix a hole in drywall

Minor surface damage can be rectified using standard filling techniques, but larger holes that have broken through into the cavity behind the drywall (for example when wall fixings have been removed or perhaps a mishap while moving large items of furniture) require the application of a backing piece to seal the hole and to prevent the filler from falling into the cavity.

TRY IT

Think pink

Use color-indicator filling products. These are pink in color when first applied, and turn white when dry enough to sand. Easy!

1. Cut a drywall patch 1 in (25 mm) longer than the hole and just wide enough to pass through it. Drill a small hole in the center of the patch with the gray side facing, and pass one end of a 6 in (150 mm) length of string through it. Tie a large knot in the string at the back of the patch, or tie it around a small panel nail, to prevent it pulling through.

2. Apply adhesive to the edges of the patch, then carefully pass it through the hole. Adjust the position of the patch so that the hole is covered and there are no gaps. Tug firmly on the string now to press the patch securely against the back of the damaged area. Allow the adhesive to set.

3. Using a joint knife apply a spackling compound to the patched area, and then snip off the string. Fill the hole almost flush with the surrounding surface. Allow to dry and add a final thin layer to bring the patched area completely flush. Use the flexible blade to smooth the surface as much as possible, then sand to a fine finish with abrasive paper or an electric sander when completely dry.

80 Patching up: spacklings and caulks

There are many patching compounds at the hardware store, but you don't need them all! This guide identifies three of the most useful and where to use them. Remember all spackling must be allowed to dry completely then sanded down for a smooth finish.

TYPE OF FILLER	SUITABLE FOR	PROS	CONS	NOTES
Ready-mixed spackling	Small surface imperfections, such as cracks and holes.	• Very easy to use. • Available in a variety of different-sized tubs.	• A soft spreading consistency that dries out slowly. • It contracts a little upon contact with air.	Always remember to replace the top of the tub or tube or it'll harden and be useless.
Powdered spackling	Filling deep holes or cracks, or where lots of filling is required.	• Drys quickly. • Good value for money.	• Must be carefully mixed to the correct consistency by adding water.	You must remember to keep the powder in the box dry, because it will set like rock.
Acrylic caulk	Filling fine or larger cracks that appear between a wall and base board, or around door or window frames.	• A flexible acrylic product, usually contained in a large tube, or cartridge inserted into a caulk gun with a trigger action. • Nozzle may be cut to deliver a particular diameter bead.	• Not suitable for rectifying imperfections in large flat surfaces such as walls or ceilings.	May be painted over when dry. You can't sand caulk when it's dry, so make sure it's smooth before it sets.

81 Easy method for filling holes or cracks

Inadequate filling and sanding is frequently the cause of poor finished results whether painting or papering. You can be assured that any lumps and bumps that you neglected to smooth away will stand out like a sore thumb when the job is completed. Recite again the DIY mantra "preparation pays"; it really is worth it.

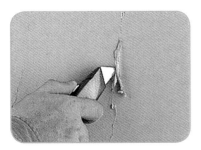

1. Examine all surfaces carefully and identify areas to be filled. Using the blade of a utility knife or a small chisel and a lightweight hammer, rake out any debris or loose surface matter from cracks or holes, then use a paintbrush to remove dust particles. Wet the edges of the damaged area with water in preparation for the spackling.

2. Using a suitable patching compound, apply filling to the crack or hole with the blade of a joint knife. The blade is quite flexible, allowing the patching compound to be squeezed into the crack or hole with a little pressure, and then be smoothed out reasonably flush with the surrounding surface. Don't be tempted to try this with an ordinary kitchen knife or another substitute; it won't do the job properly!

3. Allow the patching compound to dry completely before attempting to sand. Sanding is always a time-consuming job, but it is really worth the effort. You could use an electric sander to start with, but for the best finish, a single sheet of fine sandpaper rubbed on gently by hand will allow you to feel the smoothness of the repair.

Surface preparation: stripping wallpaper

Stripping wallpaper can be a daunting task for those new to DIY, especially if your rooms are large. However, before you can apply new paper, all old wallcoverings must be removed. Never attempt to apply new paper over old! It really is worth spending a little time and effort to ensure you create a sound surface ready for redecoration. The general idea is to dissolve the adhesive that holds the paper to the wall in order to facilitate removal; that's done either with water or with steam.

82 Choose your stripping method

The method you decide to use depends on what you have to deal with. Here's a tip: Splash a little water on the wall and see what happens! If the water soaks in, then it's just standard wallpaper (the easiest to remove); if the water runs off, then your wallpaper is the vinyl-coated variety, or perhaps covered with a few paint layers (a little more effort will be required). Multiple paper layers or thick overpainting means you're going to have to work harder.

TRY IT

Good old soap and water

If you choose the water and sponge method of applying moisture, add a squirt of dishwashing liquid to the bucket after you've filled it. The detergent helps the water stick to the paper rather than running off into puddles on the floor.

83 Removing standard wallpaper

Start by scoring the surface of the paper in order to allow moisture to penetrate through to the paste. You can crosshatch the surface using a scraper blade, but the best and quickest way is to use an orbital scorer (see panel opposite). Run the tool over the wall in a random fashion to create hundreds of tiny holes in the surface, allowing water/steam to penetrate.

YOU WILL NEED
- Orbital scorer (optional)
- Bucket
- Large sponge
- Flexible scraper
- Detergent
- Steam stripper (optional)
- Garbage bags

1. Applying the moisture: The simplest method is to soak the paper with warm water using a large sponge. The quickest and easiest way is to use a steam stripper, which looks rather like a steam-powered vacuum cleaner! The water reservoir creates steam, which is applied to the wall via a flat plate (after scoring). The paper will soften and bubble after about 30 seconds, allowing easy removal using the flat blade of a scraper.

2. Removing the paper: Use the flexible scraper to remove the damp paper, working on small sections at a time. Keep the angle of the blade quite shallow to prevent gouging out chunks of the wall underneath. When all the paper has been removed, wash down the walls with a sponge and a solution of detergent and water to dissolve paste residue.

84 Removing vinyl wallpaper

It is possible to peel away the top layer of vinyl-coated wallpaper revealing the lining paper layer underneath, which can be removed as shown left (Removing standard wallpaper). Carefully pick away at a corner at the lower edge of each drop and gently pull away the strip working from bottom to top. If you're lucky, the pieces will come off in one go.

86 Worst wallpaper offenders

- **Painted woodchip:** Woodchip wallpaper has its merits in that it's cheap, thick, durable and covers up a multitude of sins if the walls are very uneven. However it isn't very attractive and its durability makes removal a more difficult task. Make sure to score well and to apply plenty of steam or water so the paper is really soft, ready for removal with a scraper.

- **Multiple layers:** Older properties can suffer from this problem. Home improvers from previous generations may have been happy to paper then paint, repaper then repaint many times over the years, resulting in a thick multilayered barrier between you and the wall. The best way is to score, steam and strip through the layers one by one until you reach the wall beneath – a lot of effort but worth doing well.

85 Tools for the job: flexible scraper vs. orbital scorer

FLEXIBLE SCRAPER	ORBITAL SCORER
Inexpensive and multipurpose; can be used for scoring, removing old wallpaper, filling surface imperfections and scraping off paint.	The largest orbital scorers can be expensive and can only be used for scoring wallpaper.
Hand tool with no moving parts. It is slim and fits neatly into your toolbox.	Hand tool with sharp spiked wheels on the underside. It is quite bulky and almost never fits neatly anywhere!
Useful for scoring through several layers of wallpaper at once.	The rotating wheels have rows of small spikes, so cannot pierce very thick layers.
A scraper is held at a shallow angle to the wall and used to scratch through the wallpaper in a crosshatched pattern.	Very easy to use, simply place the scorer onto the wall and press gently so the spiked wheels penetrate the paper. Run the tool over the wall in a random fashion to create hundreds of tiny holes, thus allowing water or steam to penetrate, facilitating easy removal.
Care must be taken to apply the correct pressure – too much and the surface of the wall beneath the paper may be damaged.	Orbital scorers seldom damage wall surfaces if used correctly.
Suitable for flat or raised/embossed wallpapers.	Works best for smooth wallpapers, but can be used for papers with a raised pattern.
A handy tool when scoring and removing paper from small spaces or tight corners.	The smallest orbital scorer has a palm-sized area on the underside so it can be difficult to access small tight areas.
Best used for scoring small areas.	Useful for scoring large areas quickly.
Best used in conjunction with a steam stripper.	Best used in conjunction with a steam stripper.

FIX IT

It's in the bag

Always use a dust sheet to cover the floor, and place stripped paper in a garbage bag as you go because the damp paste dries quite quickly and will stick to everything it touches.

Surface preparation: ceilings

The ceiling has to be the most tiring and awkward area to repair, prepare and decorate – mainly because it is high above your head, making access difficult. It may be tempting to ignore it, but when the rest of the room is freshly decorated ceiling imperfections will really stand out. It's worth making the extra effort to ensure your home looks its best.

87   Preparing drywall ceilings

Follow the same surface preparation methods as for walls (see page 54) – the only difference is that it's more difficult, as you'll be up a ladder with your arms above your head. Make sure to work on small areas at a time, and never reach over too far when up a ladder. It's a tiring job, so try to rest between sessions of activity.

FIX IT

Ceiling "pops"

A "popped" nail is a fairly common occurrence in drywall ceilings. It is simply a protruding nail head that has worked loose from the overhead ceiling joist and popped through the surface of the drywall. It will look like a small bump, a crescent-shaped crack or a small circle of bare plaster where the paint or drywall has popped right off. Here's how to fix it and make sure it doesn't happen again.

YOU WILL NEED
- Nail punch
- Hammer
- Drywall nails or screws
- Filling knife
- Filling compound
- Sandpaper
- Touch-up paint and brush

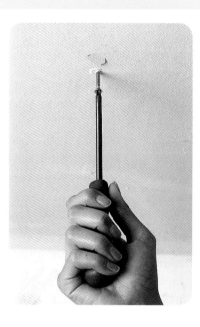

1. Use the nail punch and hammer to re-drive the old nails or, if they are protruding a lot, remove them. Place the cupped point of the nail punch over the popped nail head and tap firmly back into the joist so the head lies just below the surface.

2. To ensure the nails stay put, drive a drywall nail or screw into the joist about 2 in (5 cm) either side of the "pop." Drywall screws will countersink themselves. If you are using nails, drive nail heads below the surface as before.

3. Using a filling knife, squeeze filling compound into the surface holes, then use the flexible blade to scrape off any excess, bringing the repair flush with the surrounding ceiling.

4. When the filler is completely dry, sand smooth and apply a coat of touch-up paint to match the original.

FIX IT

Dealing with water stains and mold

- **Stains**: Plumbing leaks from overhead pipes can cause staining on ceilings, and this tends to bleed through to new paint or wallpaper. Use a stain-blocking paint before decorating, available in brush and spray form.

- **Mold:** Hot air and steam rise, so if there is inadequate ventilation the ceiling may get damp and encourage mold growth. Wash down with sugar soap (or trisodium phosphate), then when dry apply a fungicide solution to the affected area.

88   Addressing peeling paint

In high humidity areas such as kitchens and bathrooms ceiling paint may begin to peel and flake. This is usually due to poor initial application, but can be remedied by rubbing down the old paint, and re-priming the surface with a good-quality, stain-blocking primer. Repaint with specially formulated bathroom and kitchen paint when the primer coat is dry.

89 Repairing lath and plaster ceilings

Older houses are constructed with lath and plaster ceilings. Thin battens or laths are nailed to the ceiling joists then covered with a layer of plaster. How a hole is filled will depend on its size. First coat exposed laths with PVA adhesive to promote filler adherence, then fill with plaster. If the laths are broken and the hole is less than 3 in (76 mm) across, simply scrunch up some newspaper to pack the hole, then fill with plaster. For holes more than 3 in (76 mm) across, use the following method.

YOU WILL NEED

- Old paintbrush
- Safety goggles
- Dust mask
- Tin snips
- Expanded metal mesh
- Bolster chisel
- Hammer
- Plaster filler
- Plaster float
- Sandpaper

Bolster chisel

Tin snips

1. Use an old paintbrush to remove any dust and debris from the areas to be repaired, wearing safety goggles and a dust mask.

2. If the laths are damaged, use tin snips to trim the expanded metal mesh to size. The mesh will create a backing for the filler. Fit the mesh in place by curling the edges around the back of the laths.

3. Use a bolster chisel and hammer to undercut the edges of the hole so that the plaster will have a better grip. Do this gently to avoid further damage. Once again, use the old paintbrush to remove any debris.

4. Place plaster filler onto a float and push it up into the repair until it is flat against the ceiling, forcing the filler through the holes in the mesh; slide the float over the repair. Scrape off as much excess filler as you can and if necessary sand smooth when the filler is dry.

Surface preparation: woodwork

Woodwork is usually the last item on the decorator's long order of work list (see page 42), and by this time your patience and energy levels may be getting low. But remember, a well-prepared surface ensures a better, more professional-looking result, so it's really worth the effort to do the job properly. Usually woodwork is painted with a high-gloss or a semi-gloss finish – traditionally alkyd or oil-based paints were favored – but more recently latex or water-based alternatives have been preferred, due to their shorter drying times and low odor.

90 The easy way to prepare woodwork

If you're lucky, your woodwork will be in perfect condition, beautifully painted and undamaged.

YOU WILL NEED
- Sugar soap (or trisodium phosphate) and sponge
- Abrasive paper and sanding block

1. It is a relatively simple task to wash down the woodwork with a solution of sugar soap (or trisodium phosphate) and water to remove any accumulated grease and dirt, working from top to bottom. Allow to dry.

2. Rub the painted surface with abrasive paper to create a good key ready for repainting. Even if the door looks good, if you don't key the surface properly the paint won't adhere and will flake or crack. Wipe away any dust with a damp cloth.

91 Creating a key

Keying a surface means rubbing it with abrasive paper to remove the top layer. On a previously painted surface the glossy top layer is removed, providing a slightly rough surface and giving the new paint a more successful bond.

TRY IT

It's a wrap

If you have lots of flat planes to rub down, wrap a piece of abrasive paper around a cork sanding block, or make your own using a 4 in x 2 in (10 cm x 5 cm) length of timber. The block provides a nice flat surface with which to key your woodwork. Use a sanding sponge for complicated moldings.

92 Dealing with chipped paint

If the original paint job is chipped, you must fix it or it will show through and spoil the topcoat. Gently brush or sand away any loose paint surrounding the chip. Apply a little filler to the damaged area if the paint is thick, then sand smooth. If the paint layer is thin, simply apply a touch-up coat of primer to the bare wood in the chipped area, then apply a few more coats to bring the repair flush with the original.

93 The hard way to prepare woodwork

Most home decorators aren't that lucky and will have to prepare woodwork the hard way. You'll need to wash the surface with sugar soap (or trisodium phosphate) first, then rub down using abrasive paper wrapped around a sanding block.

YOU WILL NEED

- Sugar soap (or trisodium phosphate) and sponge
- Abrasive paper and sanding block
- Scraper
- Filling knife
- Filler
- Lint-free cloth
- Mineral spirits or denatured alcohol
- Paintbrush

1. If old paint has bubbled or is flaking off, push the blade of a scraper under the loose paint and lift it off carefully. Scrape or brush away any surrounding areas of flaking paint.

2. Use a small tub or tube of ready-mixed filler for small jobs. Load up the filling knife with filler and push it down into any damaged areas. Press down and draw the knife across the repair before lifting the blade off.

FIX IT

Knotty issues

When you have sanded down woodwork or stripped off the paint down to the bare wood, you may find a knot or two. These are not generally a problem, but sometimes resins from knots can bleed through to the surface of new paint and create a stain. To fix this, apply a coat of knotting solution to the stain and allow to dry before applying primer and a topcoat of paint. This will seal the knot and prevent staining.

3. Allow the filler to dry completely, then sand the filled area level with the surrounding paint job, using fine abrasive paper wrapped around a sanding block or a sanding sponge for moldings. Fine details can be sanded by folding the abrasive paper to a point or edge.

4. Finally, use a lint-free cloth (cheesecloth is ideal) soaked in mineral spirits or denatured alcohol to clean off any dust that has accumulated around the area or repair. Allow the woodwork to dry, then draw your fingers over any filled areas to make sure they are smooth. Re-sand if necessary, then wipe clean again in preparation for priming and painting the woodwork.

WALLPAPER KNOW-HOW

How to choose wallpaper

94 Wallpaper is wonderful stuff, and it provides the home decorator with an excellent opportunity to make a spectacular statement throughout the home, whether it's a feature wall, a whole room or an entrance hall. There is a mind-boggling amount of choices out there, so before you decide, there are a few things to bear in mind; some are practical and some are purely aesthetic and a matter of personal preference. Where will you put it? What is the function of the room? What style? The list can be endless, and that's even before we start thinking about colors!

WHY PAPER?

95

- The choice is vast! There are hundreds of patterns, textures, styles, color combinations and finishes to choose from.
- Wallpaper is an easy way to combine pattern and texture with flat paint finishes.
- If your walls are sound but very uneven, a good-quality, heavy-duty patterned paper is a better choice than a paint finish. The pattern will disguise the surface blemishes beautifully.
- Whatever your taste is, you can be assured there'll be a paper to suit.

- It's quick! The trend for fancy paint finishes has waned a little; however, wallpaper is a good option if you want to add pattern, texture and color at the same time.
- Wallpaper is perfect for adding texture to a flat surface.
- Think about optical illusions and the effect on space.
- While color is a pretty good reflection of your personality, a quirky wallpaper can really shout it from the rooftops.

Style choices

Use the internet to seek out some inspiration! Check DIY blog pages for trending themes. **96**

Not sure where to start? Pick an item that you love in a certain style that you like, for example, a throw pillow, a painting or a decorative ceramic piece, and work around it.

✳ **Contemporary:** An opportunity to try bold geometric patterns, floral designs, metallic effects or bright color combinations.

✳ **Retro/vintage:** There's plenty of scope for those seeking to re-create 50s, 60s, 70s style. It is rarely possible to find enough vintage wallpaper to cover a whole room, but try searching out some authentic wallpaper to use as an accent.

✳ **Romantic:** Pretty floral designs work well with damask patterns in muted tones and pastel shades.

✳ **Traditional:** Think luxury mansions! Co-ordinate grand floral designs with elegant stripes.

✳ **Country:** Farmhouse, rustic, French, Scandinavian, Shaker, Mediterranean, Moroccan ... a chance to explore styles from all over the world. Take your pick.

✳ **Minimalist:** Choose monochromatic color schemes, or bold color-block accents.

WEAR-AND-TEAR CONSIDERATIONS

Living rooms Though the living room can be considered a high-traffic area in some households, you might want to think of a reasonably hardwearing wallpaper choice for the majority of the wall area, with a contrast for a chimney breast, which is unlikely to get scuffed with furniture.

Kitchens/bathrooms A washable finish is a must here. Think about condensation and water splashes.

Bedrooms You could opt for a more luxurious quality wallpaper here, and consider accent walls for a dramatic effect.

Children's rooms Durability and washability are key points to remember.

Utility areas Some wallpapers are designed to withstand frequent scrubbing.

Hallways/stairs These high-traffic areas often get scuffed and scratched. Choose a durable paper that will withstand tough treatment.

97

TOP BUYING TIPS

98

1. Take a trip around the wallpaper section in the hardware store and pick up lots and lots of samples before you buy. Take them home and put them all over the place just to get a feel for how they might look on a chimney breast, next to a window or in combination with another paper or feature that you have already.

2. Try different colorways of the same pattern, and play around with different combinations. Wallpaper can be a major purchase so you don't want to make costly mistakes.

3. When buying wallpaper, make sure that all the batch numbers match as there can be minor color variations between batches. If you're combining papers make sure they have the same qualities, e.g. washability – especially useful when decorating kitchens or bathrooms!

4. Measure your room carefully and don't forget to allow extra for pattern matching (see Estimating quantities guide, page 48).

5. Using oversized patterns can be wasteful, as the pattern repeat will need to be matched. Always consider this when purchasing.

6. Don't forget your budget. It's easy to get carried away; do the math first before you commit to purchase.

7. Use scrubbable wallcoverings for children's rooms and high-traffic, child, pet or dirt areas!

8. New to wallpapering? Avoid buying small intricate designs with offset repeat patterns. Matching up the repeats can be difficult.

Pick your spot

99

• You don't have to hang the same wallpaper on every wall. In fact, you don't have to paper all four walls.

• Choose a bold pattern for a feature wall, a chimney breast behind a bed or in alcoves.

• Try mixing and matching different colors and patterns – try lots of samples first!

• Cover all four walls with the same paper for simplicity, but choose patterns carefully, as oversized designs can be overwhelming.

• Chair rails and picture rails provide perfectly defined areas for color and contrasts. Choose co-ordinating patterns or colors above and below the rails to create unique effects.

PATTERN PERFECT

100

• Consider optical illusions – vertical stripes can give the appearance of height, while horizontal stripes can make a room look wider.

• Very large patterns can overwhelm a small space. The general rule of thumb is big space, big pattern; small space, smaller pattern.

• Small patterns can look busy, especially if you have lots of pictures on the walls or ornaments.

• Light colors can appear to open up smaller spaces, while dark colors have the opposite effect.

• Big bold patterns are very popular, but you have to be sure your room can handle it; patterns can look very different in situ and in different light.

WALLPAPER OPTIONS

101

» LINING PAPER is a plain natural-colored wallcovering used as a base for decorative wallpaper, or to create a smooth surface for painting. As a rule, lining paper is hung horizontally so the seams don't show when decorative wallpaper is pasted on top.

» WOODCHIP wallpaper looks like lining paper with small woodchips in the surface. It can be a decorator's nightmare if you need to remove it, but it has its good qualities; it's cheap, durable and when painted adds an unobtrusive surface texture. It also covers lots of surface defects in the wall underneath.

» EMBOSSED wallpaper has a raised pattern or texture and is ideal to use alone or as a base for a paint color. Be careful because even a seemingly random texture will have a pattern repeat, so you might have to do some matching.

» WASHABLE wallpapers have a transparent plastic coating applied over the printed pattern. This coating is designed to resist staining and moisture, and can be wiped clean using a damp cloth or sponge. However, you cannot paint over this type of wallpaper as it resists paint too!

» VINYL-COATED wallpapers consist of a paper backing layer then a patterned vinyl layer. Easy to hang and strip off, and easy to wipe clean; a good choice for high-moisture areas such as kitchens and bathrooms.

» FLOCK wallpaper has moved from the restaurant and into the most stylish of homes. These papers generally have a plain background and a raised pattern that feels like velvet to the touch. Be warned that these delicate papers are not for use in high-traffic areas.

» SPECIALTY FINISHES – there are lots available: suede effects, or metallic overprints. These can be a little tricky to hang and cannot be painted over.

» HAND-PRINTED wallpapers are the pinnacle of wallcoverings. Very expensive, but very lovely if you want to make a real statement and have the budget to match.

3 Walls, ceilings and floors

Walls and ceilings are probably the first surfaces you'll be decorating, with floors following closely behind. While each element requires a slightly different approach and method, it's worth considering these areas as parts of a whole; think about how the different planes will work together. If you're looking to make a quick decorating fix or a major refurbishment, this chapter will show you how — the dos and the don'ts, and lots of handy tips, tricks and techniques to make your decorating task easy.

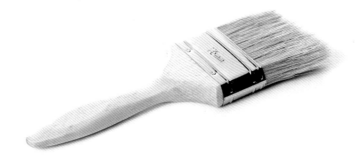

Making good

Basic surface preparation is a standard procedure at the start of any decorating process (see pages 54–61). The best-case scenario will present as a few cracks and holes to be filled and some woodwork to rub down. However, if you're doing lots of decorating or a complete house remodel, then you're likely to be removing fixings or pulling out cupboards. You might be surprised at what you find. Doing repairs takes time, but don't be tempted to cut corners.

102 Tackling cracks

There are two types of cracks to watch out for – structural and superficial.

• **Professional fix** Structural cracks are large, deep and will probably be wider at one end than at the other. If you spot any of these, seek advice from a professional. There may be subsidence or other structural issues, and these should not be tackled by the home decorator.

• **Easy fix (walls and ceilings)** Superficial cracks are shallow, hairline surface disruptions, sometimes caused by settlement or drying of plaster. These are an easy fix for the home decorator; time-consuming but not difficult.

• **Easy fix (wood)** Minor cracks and opened grain may be caused by wear and tear, splits around nail holes or simply drying out. These can be repaired by wood filler, but if the timber is beyond filling then you'll need to replace it.

103 Neat fix for a hole in plaster

If the hole is not too large, but quite deep, piling on the filler sometimes doesn't work. Instead press a ball of wet newspaper into the hole to fill the majority of the void, then apply filler over the top.

TRY IT

Reusing old wall fixings

If you want to reuse your wall fixings and don't want to lose their position under layers of wallpaper, simply place a matchstick or toothpick in the screw hole so it protrudes slightly from the wall – it will poke through the wallpaper.

104 Paint problems

As paint ages and wears you may be faced with a few problems to sort out before you begin applying fresh topcoats. The problem may be related to the surface underneath the old paint finish. Never paint over flaking, bubbling surfaces; instead sand down to a sound surface and then repaint.

MATERIAL	PROBLEM	CAUSE	FIX
Wood	Repeated blistering or discoloration.	May indicate a knot underneath that is bleeding resin.	Remove blistered paint, apply knotting solution to knot and repaint.
Wood	Crazing	Topcoat incompatible with undercoat.	Sand back to the wood, prime and repaint.
Plaster, drywall	Crazing	Paint was applied before plaster was completely dry.	Sand down to the plaster and repaint.

Filling gaps and crevices

Gaps can appear anywhere and everywhere – between woodwork and the wall, around doors and windows, cornices where ceilings meet walls or along the top of base boards. This is where a tube of sealant and a cartridge gun will turn into your best friend; simply squeeze a bead of filler into the crack.

105 Hiding old wall fixings

If you have removed wall-mounted fixtures or furnishings and are left with screw holes with screw anchors inside, do not be tempted to fill over them.

• If you can get a grip on it, carefully draw the anchor out of the wall using needle-nosed pliers.

• Alternatively, replace the screw in the anchor, then grip the screw head with the pliers and pull it out of the wall.

• If by this time you're left with a big hole, squirt some quick-setting filler into the hole, leaving it a little raised from the surface. When dry, sand smooth.

• If you're left with a really big hole, you will need something more substantial to fill it. Get some wooden dowel fixings to match the diameter of the hole and fit snugly inside. Tap the dowel right down into the hole, then fill over the top.

Painting over wallpaper

Redecorating doesn't necessarily mean stripping back to the bare bones and starting from scratch. You may just want to make a well-wallpapered room good enough to repaint. Here's how to do it:

YOU WILL NEED
• Flexible filling knife
• Wallpaper adhesive
• Utility knife
• Paintbrush
• Sugar soap (or trisodium phosphate)
• Bucket and sponge

1. For lifting seams or corners, spread a little wallpaper paste underneath using the filling knife. Press the back into place.

2. For air bubbles, make two slits in the form of a cross in each bubble with a utility knife. Carefully peel back the four triangular tabs, and apply wallpaper paste behind each one. Press the tabs back into place.

3. Finally, a quick wash-down using a solution of sugar soap (or trisodium phosphate) and water will remove dust or grease buildup. Let dry, then apply the new paint.

106 Can it be painted?

Paper you can paint over:
• Woodchip
• Lining paper
• Anaglypta
• Relief pattern
• Plain or patterned wallpaper

Paper you can't paint over:
• Washable wallpaper
• Paper that has been painted over many times, or has a gloss finish
• Vinyl-coated paper, unless the vinyl layer can be peeled away
• Flock-printed wallpaper
• Wallpaper with a metallic finish

Tiling basics

Tiling is a relatively easy job for the home decorator – if your walls are sound and flat, it is a case of applying adhesive, pressing the tiles into position and then grouting the gaps. Wall tiles are small and easy to handle, and adhesives are strong enough to hold tiles securely to most surfaces. The practicalities of cutting, shaping and getting the lines straight might prove tricky, but practice makes perfect.

107   Make a tile gauge

To plan the layout of the tiles you will need to make a tile gauge. Use a 3 ft (1 m) length 1 in x 2 in (25 mm x 50 mm) planed piece of softwood that has a smooth straight edge. Lay several tiles on a flat surface using spacers between each one to allow for the grout. Use a pencil to mark off the widths along the wood.

108   Planning the tile layout

Because ceramic tiles are a fixed size, you can use their measurements to calculate how many complete tiles you can use to cover an area and work out how many cut tiles you'll need to fit around the edges. Use a tile gauge to make the job easier.

1. Hold the gauge horizontally against the bottom of a wall/window to work out where the whole tiles will fall. Adjust it so that the pieces at the ends will be of equal size. Try to center the layout around an obstacle such as a window. Cut equal-sized pieces to position on each side of the obstacle.

2. If you center the gauge and find that you will be cutting narrow strips of tile (less than a quarter of the tile width), move the gauge along by half a tile's width to increase the size of a cut tile. Narrow strips can be difficult to cut.

3. Repeat the process on the vertical plane. This process will tell you how many tiles will be required for each row and column. Always count cut tiles as whole. Multiply the number of rows and columns together to calculate the total number of tiles required.

109 Plotting the tiles

It would be unusual for a tiling job to use complete tiles only; most areas will require cut tiles somewhere in order to fit the space properly. Measure your area accurately, then make a sketch plan to help decide where and what size the cut tiles will be. Mark your guidelines on the walls using a pencil.

TRY IT

Making plans

Draw sketch plans to scale on squared paper to make the planning and calculating a little easier. It may take several attempts to get the plan right, but don't start tiling or cutting until you know exactly what you're doing.

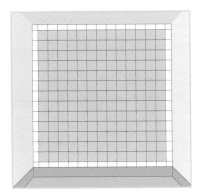

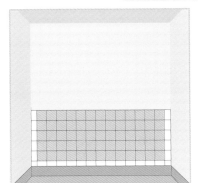

Plan to use as many whole tiles as possible to fill the space, centering them so there are equal distances left at each side. A plain wall without any obstructions should have cut tiles of equal size positioned at the outer edges or in corners.

When planning a partially tiled wall, use whole tiles at the top edge, perhaps finished with a row of chair-profile tiles. Any cut tiles should be positioned at the lower and outer edges. Rooms are rarely square, so cutting to fit may be a challenge.

If tiling is required around a window, it is best to center the tiles around it, as it will be the major feature in the room. This may mean that you have to cut tiles of uneven widths at the ends of the rows and columns.

110 Getting the walls ready

In order that tile adhesive sticks to the wall, you must first remove any wallpaper or old tiles, and sand down any painted surfaces using coarse abrasive paper and a sanding block. Wash the walls with a solution of sugar soap (or trisodium phosphate) and water to remove dust, dirt or wallpaper adhesive residue. Repair any surface blemishes, and seal new plaster with a primer of water-based paint.

TRY IT

Tiling over paint

Not all painted walls can be tiled. The best way to test the surface is to stick a piece of adhesive tape on it and leave it overnight. Pull the tape off the next day; if the paint comes off with it, then the paint must be stripped, because the tile adhesive won't stick and the tiles will fall off.

111 How to remove old wall tiles

Removing old tiles requires a bolster chisel, a heavy club hammer – and a lot of hard work. Remember your safety gear: gloves and goggles.

1. Place the bolster chisel in the center of one tile and hit it hard with a club hammer, which will shatter the tile. Insert the chisel into one of the cracks and gently tap it further, then use it to lever off the pieces of tile.

2. To remove the remaining tiles, insert the bolster chisel under one edge of an adjacent tile and gently hammer it in before levering off the tile. Some will come away whole, and others will break into pieces. Try not to damage the wall surface as you work.

Tile cutting and application

The most important thing to remember when tiling a room is that walls, floors and corners are seldom square and should not be used as guides to assess a true horizontal or vertical plane. Instead, fix horizontal and vertical guide battens to each wall, positioned in accordance with the starting points you have planned using your tile gauge. However if you are tiling above a bathtub or kitchen countertop that you know to be level, there is no need to use guide battens. The first row of tiles can be set immediately on top.

112 Using guide battens

It's good practice to use guide battens to ensure that your rows are horizontal and your columns are vertical. You can't successfully do this by eye alone.

YOU WILL NEED
- Drill
- Softwood battens
- Masonry nails
- Spirit level
- Hammer

1. Pre-drill holes in your horizontal guide batten to take the masonry nails. Hold the batten in place, following the marks made previously when using the tile gauge. Use a spirit level to ensure the batten is truly horizontal. Drive the nails in partway, leaving the nail heads proud to facilitate easy removal later.

2. Fit a second batten in place at one end of the area to be tiled, at right angles to the first horizontal batten, to act as a vertical guide to the edge column of tiles. Attach vertical and horizontal guide battens to other walls being tiled.

113 Perfect results with a tile-cutting jig

You will achieve the best results, and fewer breakages, if you use a platform tile-cutting jig instead of a pencil-point tile cutter and a tile snapper. A tile cutter is most useful when cutting large tiles.

1. First measure and mark the tile accurately using a ruler and a chinagraph or wax pencil.

2. Lay the tile squarely on the platform cutter, aligning the marked line with the overhead track that holds the blade.

3. Using the handle, gently lower the blade so it sits on the marked cutting line. Press the blade and push it forward in one smooth, firm and steady action. The blade will score a line along the surface of the tile.

4. Now pull the handle back and place the two prongs on the underside of the handle on either side of the scored line.

5. Press the handle down onto the tile firmly to snap the tile cleanly along the scored line.

114 Field and corner tiles

The word "field" refers to all of the whole tiles that cover the area; it is good practice to lay all the field tiles first. Any tiles that lie in the corners or around the edges of the field are laid last and usually require careful cutting or trimming to size.

YOU WILL NEED
- Tile adhesive
- Notched adhesive spreader
- Tiles
- Tile spacers (if not using self-spacing tiles)
- Tile-cutting jig

TRY IT

Using mosaics

Mosaic tiles use the same adhesive as standard tiles. Simply press the tile side of the mosaic sheet onto a bed of adhesive, allowing grouting space between the sheets. Trim off smaller strips of tile to fit corners and obstacles. When the adhesive is dry, moisten the paper backing with water and remove. Grout the tiles to finish the job.

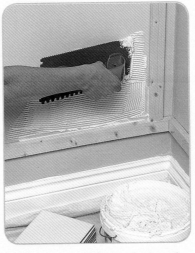

1. Scoop out some of the tile adhesive and spread a band of it on the wall a little wider than the height of the first row of tiles, starting at the lower corner created by the guide battens. Press the teeth of the spreader against the wall to leave even ridges of adhesive.

2. Rest the edge of the first tile on the horizontal batten, align it with the vertical one and press it into the adhesive. Working horizontally, press the next tile into place. Butt together tiles that have tile-spacing lugs; use plastic tile spacers between each tile for standard square-edged tiles. Continue the process until all the whole tiles are in place.

3. You will now need to remove the vertical guide battens and cut the first edge tile to size (see opposite page for using a tile-cutting jig). Set each cut tile in place by spreading adhesive on the back of the tile instead of the wall. Continue cutting and setting each tile one at a time.

4. After completing the tile columns up the side edge of the wall, remove the horizontal guide battens. To fit a tile into a corner you may have to cut it to size both vertically and horizontally. Allow the adhesive to dry completely before applying grout or sealant.

If you have large areas to tile and lots of cutting to do, then it is probably a good idea to rent a heavy-duty diamond tile cutter. Remember to wear your safety gear and practice with a few spare tiles before you begin. A machine like this will save time and reduce breakages.

Tiling around corners and obstacles

Most rooms have corners and other obstacles such as windows, doors, water pipes and plug sockets to negotiate. The procedure here is to set as many whole tiles around the obstacle as possible and then trim, drill or cut tiles one at a time to fit. Cutting complicated shapes can be difficult, so make sure you have plenty of extra tiles to allow for breakages and errors. Practice on spare pieces of cut tile.

115   Negotiating doors

- If the door is in the center of a wall and you are tiling to ceiling level, center the tile layout to avoid ending up with narrow pieces alongside the door and at the corners.

- If the door is in the corner of a room, set out the two walls in the normal way, then cut tiles into the area above the door to complete floor-to-ceiling tiling.

116   How to trim narrow strips

If you have to trim off a narrow strip, make a score line using a tile cutter and then nibble away the waste using a tile nipper. Use a tile file to smooth off the cut edge neatly.

FIX IT

Pipework and obstacles

Kitchens and bathrooms invariably contain a selection of pipes and awkward shapes. It will help to cut a tile-sized paper template and sketch a shape that fits around the obstacle. Transfer the outline to the tile using a wax pencil, then drill and cut to follow the shape using tile nippers, a tile saw or a drill. In order to accommodate large obstacles it is better to position the tiles so the join is halfway along the obstacle's shape. This is easier than cutting a shape from the middle of a tile.

117   Mitering border tiles

Border tiles add a decorative element to tiled areas and provide a neat edge to a backsplash or along the top edge of a bathtub or shower panel. Center whole tiles along the top, then cut diagonal miters to fit the corners.

YOU WILL NEED
- Border tiles
- Wax pencil
- Tile saw
- Workbench
- Tile file
- Clamp

At the corner, the tip of the miter will extend beyond the tiled area. Mark the measurement at the top and bottom of the tile, then cut using a tile saw. Cut a second miter to match, then test it in position – you may have to adjust the fit of the join using a tile file.

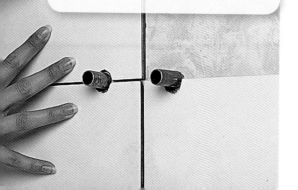

118   Perfect external corners

Negotiating external corners can be tricky because they are seldom straight or truly vertical. It will be necessary to tile each wall separately, working from horizontal guide battens, so that the columns will run true to each other. This example shows a window, but the same principles apply to doors.

YOU WILL NEED
- Tiles
- Softwood batten and nails
- Hammer
- Tile nippers
- Wax pencil
- Clamp
- Workbench
- Tile saw
- Tile scorer
- Tile file

1. If you are tiling to ceiling level, place the whole tiles up to the window, but not over the window. Fit a batten to the wall with its top edge aligned to the lowest row of whole tiles above the height of the window. The batten supports the whole tiles applied above the window.

2. Fill in the cut tiles around the window. Start near the sill, where you may have to make an L-shaped cut (see Step 4) or use tile nippers to fit the tile around the sill. Make sure you plan the tile layout in advance to avoid having to make difficult cuts.

3. Wait for the adhesive to set before removing the batten at the top of the window. Cut and set the remaining tiles to fit the narrow edges around the window. Try to avoid cutting very thin strips, as these can easily break.

4. If you have an L-shaped cut to make, mark the cutting lines on the tile using a wax pencil. Clamp the tile to a workbench then cut the first line with a tile saw. Remove the tile, then score and snap the second cut; smooth edges using a tile file.

5. Set all the whole tiles inside the window recess, working away from the external corner. If the tiles do not have spacing lugs, make sure you use tile spacers between the bottom tiles and the windowsill to allow a gap for grouting.

6. Finally, measure and cut one tile at a time to fill in the back of the window recess. Once the tile adhesive dries, usually in about four hours, you may apply grout and sealant if required.

Tiling: grouting and sealing

Once your tiling job is complete, with all the tiles neatly cut and set in position and secured with tile adhesive, the grouting can begin. An area of ceramic tiles will not be waterproof until grouted and sealed. Grout is available ready-mixed in tubes or tubs, or you can mix it yourself from powder. Most grout is white, but other colors are available to match particular color schemes or to create a contrast.

119   Tips for great grouting

- Try not to press the grout with your fingers; it can be rough and irritate the skin.

- Wear disposable latex gloves when grouting.

- Always remove excess grout before it dries.

- Use an old toothbrush to push grout into small, awkward spaces.

- Don't forget to apply grout to the top edge of a run of tiles if you are not using special border or edging tiles.

- Grout or apply sealant to edges where tiles meet door or window frames.

120   Foolproof grouting

Grout is applied in the gaps between all the tiles. It dries hard, and once dry it will provide a good seal against water penetration. Note: It is advisable to seal the wall surface before tiling to ensure a completely waterproof barrier.

YOU WILL NEED
- Bucket
- Grout spreader
- Grout
- Grout finishing tool (or dowel or other round object)
- Sponge
- Dry cloth

1. Use the grout spreader to press some grout into the gaps between the tiles, drawing the flexible rubber blade across the tiles at right angles to each grout line. Scrape away excess grout from the face of the tile as you go.

2. Draw a grout finishing tool along the grout lines to give them a neat, concave finish. Alternatively you can use a piece of dowel or other rounded object, such as a ballpoint pen top, to create the same effect.

3. Leave the grout to set, then wipe the tile surface with a clean damp sponge to remove any excess. If you are using a combined adhesive/grout, remove it when wet as it is difficult to do so when dry. Finally, use a dry cloth to buff away any powdery residue left after sponging.

121 How to use sealant

A sealant will remain flexible when dry, and so it is ideal for sealing the gap between a row of tiles and a bathtub or washbasin. Grout is too rigid to provide a waterproof joint in these places.

YOU WILL NEED
- Cartridge of silicone sealant
- Utility knife
- Cartridge gun

Note: Do not tile or seal around a plastic bathtub if it is empty, as the bathtub may distort and damage the seal when it is filled with water. Always fill the bathtub and let it drain when both grout and sealant are dry and set.

1. Cut the sealant cartridge nozzle at a 45-degree angle to give an extruded bead wide enough to bridge the gap between the bottom row of tiles and the fixture. Place the cartridge into the gun holder. Squeeze the trigger and pull the nozzle along the gap.

2. To finish the seal, draw a wet finger along the bead to achieve a smooth, concave shape. Carefully wipe away any excess sealant or smudges using a damp cloth, then let dry completely.

122 Expert silicone application

Getting a smooth, straight bead of silicone is more difficult than it looks.

- Practice on a piece of cardboard first, or in the corners of a cardboard box.

- Before starting to seal the gap, place strips of masking tape on each surface, leaving a space a little wider than the gap you need to fill. Peel the tape off when you have finished.

FIX IT

Reshaping grout

If the shaping process exposes any gaps or small holes in the grout joins between tiles, put a little grout on your fingertip and press it into place. Reshape the joint as before, using the grout shaper.

TRY IT

Using sealant strip

Instead of applying sealant to the join between tile and fixture, you can use an L-shaped adhesive plastic strip. It forms the same waterproof seal, and it is useful if the gap is large.

123 Freshening up grout

Grout can become discolored over time. If you are prepared for a lot of hard work you can remove the old stuff and apply fresh, clean grout. Or, freshen up grimy grout using a bleach solution.

124 Using epoxy grout

Epoxy grout differs from regular grout in that it is made from resins that are mixed with a filling compound and dries to form a very waterproof and durable seal between tiles. However, it can look a little like plastic when it dries and can be difficult to work with. It can be useful when installing glass tiles.

TILE KNOW-HOW

Why Choose Tiles?

- **Decorative** They come in all shapes, sizes, colors, patterns and textures.
- **Durable** Most tiles have a shiny glazed surface layer, which is very hard.
- **Washable** The glazed layer will repel grease, dirt and grime; tiles are perfect for kitchens.
- **Waterproof** The glazed layer makes tiles impervious to moisture.

125

ALL SHAPES AND SIZES

127

Square or rectangular tiles are most common, but there are other shapes such as hexagonal, octagonal, Provençal or small interlocking mosaic shapes that can be used to create interesting effects. Standard square tiles usually range from 4¼ in (11 cm) up to 12 in (30 cm), while mosaic tiles can be the size of a postage stamp. Thicknesses may vary from ⅛ in (3 mm) to ¼ in (6 mm) for wall tiles, and up to ⅜ in (10 mm) for heavy-duty floor tiles.

REVIVE GRIMY GROUT

130

Over time your nice clean grout will discolor and begin to look unsightly. Use an old toothbrush and some vinegar to remove grime and restore the whiteness. For larger areas, fill an old, dishwashing liquid bottle with vinegar and apply it to the grout lines. Allow the solution to soak into the grout for 10 or 15 minutes, and then scrub it clean.

HOW TO CHOOSE TILES

126

- ✳ **Choose what you really like**, but keep an eye on your budget. Tiles can be expensive, so it's important to make accurate estimates and do the math properly before you make your choice; even small areas can take a lot of tiles.
- ✳ **Plan the layout carefully**, as the effect of fancy motifs or patterns may be spoiled if you have lots of sockets or obstacles to consider. Smaller mosaic tiles may be a good choice in this case.
- ✳ **Where are your tiles going to be placed** – wall, backsplash or countertop? Wall tiles cannot always be used for countertops. Check the PEI standard rating (see opposite) to match the tile's durability to its intended situation and your lifestyle.

COLORED GROUT

128

Consider the color of the grout when you choose your tiles. If you're using dark-colored tiles then it would be a good idea to use black or dark grout, as a white one tends to stand out a bit too much and detract from the color or pattern of the tile.

Where to use

- Bathrooms
- Kitchens
- Coat closets
- Utility rooms

129

HOW DURABLE IS MY TILE?

131

Tiles are in general a pretty durable item, but they are not all the same; the durability of an individual tile is shown by its PEI (Porcelain Enamel Institute) rating.

PEI RATING	APPLICATIONS
1 Very light traffic	• All interior wall applications • Kitchens, bathrooms • Very light-traffic residential floors • Unsuitable for heavy or constant foot traffic
2 Light traffic	• All interior wall and countertop applications • Light-traffic residential interior floors • Unsuitable for heavy-traffic areas such as kitchens, entryways, stairs
3 Moderate traffic	• All interior wall and countertop applications • Residential floors • Suitable for kitchens and bathrooms
4 Moderate to heavy traffic	• All interior wall and countertop applications • Residential floors • Suitable for kitchens, bathrooms, utility rooms and entryways
5 Heavy traffic	• All interior wall and countertop applications • Residential floors • Suitable for heavy traffic; excellent durability

132 Tiling on existing tiles

Did you know you can tile over tiles, if the original tiled area is sound and flat and the tiles are firmly attached to the wall? You can apply new tiles in the same way as for a flat wall surface. It pays, however, to rub down the shiny surface of the old tiles using a silicon carbide abrasive paper to create a good key for the tile adhesive. Wash the keyed surface with warm soapy water, then let dry completely before adding the new tiles. Try to ensure that the new tiles overlap the old ones so the spaces between don't fall in the same place.

Mixing grout

133

If you're using powdered grout, make sure that you mix it thoroughly and achieve a nice thick but spreadable consistency. Add water bit by bit; you can always add more but you can't take it out!

REMOVING MOLD AND MILDEW

134

Mix together equal quantities of vinegar and household salt in a bowl then use the resulting solution to scrub away the moldy residue. Remember to open a window as the solution will be quite pungent!

REMOVING LIMESCALE

Limescale and mineral buildup can ruin the appearance of shiny tiled areas, resulting in gray, crusty deposits in corners and along grout lines. Use acidic liquids like white wine vinegar or lemon juice to remove the offending matter. Just apply your chosen liquid and leave it to soak into the grout for at least 30 minutes, and then scrub it clean.

135

Tile options

Standard ceramic tiles are flat clay shapes with
a color or pattern on one side that is covered
with a protective glaze. Tiles are fired to make
a hard, durable product that is waterproof and
stain resistant. The face side of the tile may be
smooth or textured. Tiles may also be made of
glass, stone or marble.

136   Tiling style

- **Half tiling** Tiling up to a height of about 4 ft (1.2 m) is a very
  economical way of introducing a tiled element to a room
  without the effect being overwhelming.

- **Backsplash** In bathrooms or kitchens, the backsplash is a
  great opportunity to add color and pattern and to create a
  decorative, easy-clean wall surface. They have to withstand
  splashes of hot water, oil, grease and cleaning fluids. They are
  usually in direct high-traffic areas because they are mostly
  used in kitchens and bathrooms. The total area probably won't
  be too large, so it won't blow the budget – an ideal opportunity
  to let your creativity flow.

- **Creativity** The variety of patterns and designs available makes
  it easy to create your own unique decorative effects. Some
  tiles fit together to form larger motifs.

- **Borders** Patterned contrast tiles can be used as friezes or
  borders for larger areas of plain-colored field tiles.

- **Mosaics** Mosaic tiles are perfect for tiling large areas because
  the grout lines help to break up the color. Note: In hard-water
  areas you may experience unsightly limescale buildup.

- **Square or rectangular tiles** These are easier to use than those
  with an irregular shape.

*Mosaic tiles echo the colors and materials of the frosted-glass
bathroom fixtures.*

*These large, rectangular ceramic tiles have a bevelled edge and
a surface design that simulates natural marble.*

TRY IT

Make the most of mosaics

An old wooden table could provide the
perfect surface for a creative mosaic project,
or a simple grid of square or rectangular
tiles. Make sure that the surface is clean and
dry, apply the grout, then press the tiles into
place using the same method as you would
if you were tiling a wall. If you decide to get
arty with a pile of mosaics then it's a good
idea to make a paper template first and
sketch your design on it. Try out a few tiles and
see how they look, then use a tile nipper to cut
them to fit if necessary. Now sketch the design
onto the table surface. For mosaic projects it is
better practice to apply the adhesive bit by bit
as you go, either to the surface or to the
back of each individual tile using a small
flexible knife. Apply grout between the
tiles when the adhesive has set.

Porcelain tiles made to look like solid wood *Opulent, large format decor tiles* *Matte and gloss glass mosaic tiles*

137 Tile types

- **Field tiles** These are used to fill in large areas, are glazed on the face and on four sides, and can be cut to size.

- **Edge/border tiles** These have one rounded or decorative edge to finish off edges and corners.

- **Spacer tiles** Many tiles have lugs built into each side, and so they are self-spacing when set out on the wall.

- **Standard tiles** Plain or patterned and usually square or rectangular in shape, these are a popular choice for most tile jobs in the kitchen and bathroom. Some are very dense and have been fired to higher temperatures for use on countertops.

- **Mosaics** These are small tiles, usually held together on a paper backing to form a sheet.

- **Inserts** A small square tile may be used with a larger tile made with one corner missing in order to accommodate the insert.

- **Hand-painted** These are unique and individual; no two hand-painted tiles will be exactly the same, and this adds to their charm. Ideal for inserts and special designs.

- **Handmade** Handcrafted tiles are unusual and create a stunning visual effect. They can vary in thickness and size, so care must be taken when applying them to walls.

- **Borders** These can be flat rectangular shapes, thin pencil tiles or narrow rope-edged feature tiles. They are generally used as edges to field tiles or to frame a design feature.

- **Insets and features** These are special tiles, usually with a raised pattern or texture, used as a visual accent.

- **Ceramic tiles** The most widely used tiles. Great for general wall applications, they can withstand heat, dirt and moisture and are easy to clean. Flat, smooth surfaces are ideal for decal and paint decoration.

- **Marble** Standard tile shapes may be made from natural marble, and are suitable for traditional or classic styles.

- **Stone** Most commonly used for countertops and floors. Natural color and texture; use smooth for countertops or textured for floors. Must be sealed, as stone is porous.

- **Glass** Mostly used for walls and backsplashes; easily recycled.

Dark tiles and white grout make a striking contrast. *Large tiles are easy to use on large areas.*

1. Floor tiles are extremely durable and easy to clean but can appear cold and harsh especially in living rooms. This ceramic option is cleverly designed to look and feel like solid wood flooring. It combines the practicality of a tile with the appearance of softness and warmth of a natural material.

2. Large patterned tiles are best utilized as a feature wall; plain tiles of a similar size and quality can be used as a contrast for the remaining wall areas. The subtle surface design creates interest without overwhelming the space.

3. Floor tiles are extremely hardwearing and easy to clean. They can be laid as a grid, perpendicular to the walls or in a diagonal pattern, or a combination of both. Remember that a pattern that requires a lot of cutting will incur a lot of wastage.

4. Mosaic tiles come in all sorts of shapes, sizes and colors. These thin rectangular tiles could be used vertically or horizontally to create different effects. The design here is very economical in that only the facing areas are covered with mosaic and the returns and unseen areas are painted with a toning paint.

Painting basics: using a brush

When all the preparation work is done, it's time to start painting. Most people reach for a paintbrush when decorating their walls or woodwork, but there are other application methods as well. Each has its merits, and some people favor one method over another, but, in general, a combination of different methods usually does the trick.

138 Brush scraper

Attach a length of wire around the handles of your paint can or paint pail. You can scrape the paintbrush against the wire instead of the edge of the container; this keeps from clogging the rim of the can and also avoids paint drips down the side.

139 How to handle a paintbrush

- Always "flirt and strop" before using a new paintbrush. "Flirt" the bristles between your fingers and "strop" the brush into the palm of your hand. This will remove any loose bristles that may spoil your paint finish.

- When using small- or medium-sized brushes, e.g. for cutting in (edging), it is best to grip the ferrule (metal part) between the fingers and thumb in order to achieve better control.

- Wider brushes used for painting large areas can be tiring to use for long periods of time. It is far more comfortable to grip these by the handle and not by the ferrule.

140 Where to use a paintbrush

Use small or angled paintbrushes for cutting in around edges or for painting areas too small for a roller. Home decorators are divided over whether a wide brush or a roller is better for filling in large wall areas. Paintbrushes can drip, whereas rollers can splatter; brushes use less paint than a roller and are easier to clean. However there's no substitute for experience, so give both a try and choose the method that suits you best.

You will have greater control of your brush by gripping the ferrule.

Covering large areas will be easier if you hold your brush by the handle.

FIX IT

Using custom-mixed paint

Paint color, especially custom-mixed paint, can vary from one can to another. If you are using more than one can for your project, this may result in a slight color variation from wall to wall. Mix the contents of the cans together in a bucket and stir thoroughly before you begin. This process is called "boxing."

141 Brush check

- Check that the metal ferrule has not rusted. Remove any rust using steel wool or abrasive paper, as the particles can discolor paint.

- Always ensure that the ferrule is firmly attached to the handle; you don't want the bristles falling into the paint can, dropping to the floor or splattering other paint job.

- Wash brushes and let them dry before beginning work. If they have been stored unwrapped they may have accumulated dust.

142 Professional paintbrushing

In order to achieve a professional finish with a brush, you need to spread the paint evenly onto the work surface without letting the paint run, drip or overlap onto other areas. Overload the brush and you are likely to create runs and drips; stretching the paint too far results in patchy coverage. You will first need to use a small brush to cut into corners and edges, then a larger brush to fill in the remaining areas.

Cutting in

1. Dip the brush into the paint, loading about one-third of its bristle length. (Dipping deeper overloads the brush.) Tap the bristles on the side of the can. Dragging the brush against the lip of the can causes the bristles to wear and clogs the lip with paint.

2. Cut into the edges using the narrow edge of the brush or a slanted brush, pressing just enough to flex the bristles. Keep an eye on the paint edge and paint with long, slow strokes. Always paint from a dry area into wet paint to avoid lap marks.

FIX IT

Mixing it up

Make sure your paint is well and truly mixed by using a variable-speed drill and a paint-mixing bit. Set the drill on a low speed and remember to switch it off before lifting the bit out of the paint. Paint can separate quickly, so regular stirring will ensure a good consistency.

Large areas

1. Use a 3 in (8 cm) or 4 in (10 cm) brush for large areas. Apply the paint with two or three diagonal strokes, holding the brush at a 45-degree angle to the wall and pressing just enough to flex the bristles. Now distribute the paint evenly with horizontal strokes.

2. Smooth out the surface by drawing the brush vertically from the top to the bottom of the painted area. Use light strokes and lift the brush from the surface at the end of each stroke. This method is best for slow-drying alkyd paints.

TRY IT

Priming bare walls

When painting bare drywall or plaster, apply a coat of primer to the entire project area and let dry before applying the paint.

Painting basics: using a roller

Paint rollers are generally used to apply water-based paint to large areas such as walls and ceilings. Choose a roller sleeve with a short pile for painting smooth plaster or drywall, a medium pile for textured wallcoverings or a long pile for deeply textured plasterwork or paint.

143   Where to use a roller

Paint rollers are ideal for applying paint to large areas quickly; they are also available in a mini size to gain access behind radiators and in other small areas. However, you cannot paint right into corners with a roller, and they can splatter if "driven" too quickly. They also use quite a lot of paint, and can be messy and time-consuming to clean.

FIX IT

Roller hazards

Ridges of paint left on the surface by the edge of the roller are called "fat edges." If you let them dry, you will then need to sand the surface smooth and repaint. Here's how to avoid common roller problems:

- Don't press too hard on the roller, as it will force more paint to the edge, creating fat edges.

- Try not to overload the roller. Paint can seep into the cover and leak out onto your surface when rolling.

- Never begin rolling close to a corner; start about 6 in (15 cm) away and work inward toward it. This avoids heavy paint buildup in the corner.

- Before you roll back over a section to smooth out the previous coat, tilt the roller slightly to apply a little pressure on the open side; this releases excess paint. Smooth by running the roller over the surface again.

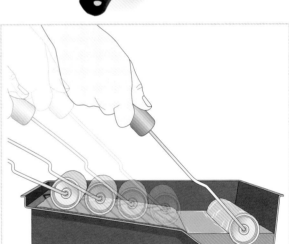

144   Ready to roll

1. Prime the roller cover with water (if using latex paint) or mineral spirits (if using alkyd paint) to remove any lint. Squeeze out the excess liquid.

2. Fill the reservoir in the roller tray with paint.

3. Dip the roller fully into the reservoir to load it with paint.

4. Lift the roller from the reservoir and roll it backward and forward on the texture ramp to distribute the paint through the pile.

5. The roller should be full but not dripping when lifted from the tray.

145 Expert rolling

Paint surfaces in small sections about 2–4 ft (60–120 cm) in size at a time, cutting in the edges and corners before filling in the main area. Roll the area while the cut-in sections are still wet, and start the next section while the edges of the first are still wet. This technique, called "painting to a wet edge," avoids unsightly lap marks on the finished surface.

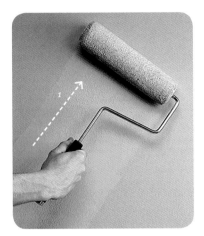

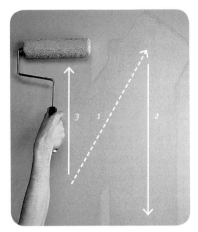

1. Take up the loaded roller and make a diagonal sweep (1) about 4 ft (120 cm) long on the surface. On walls, roll upward on the first stroke. Drive the roller slowly but firmly to avoid splatters. Rollers can often create a fine splatter pattern that seems to find its way onto every other surface in the room.

2. Draw the roller straight down (2) from the first diagonal sweep. Lift the roller from the surface, shift it to the beginning of the diagonal and roll upward (3) to complete the unloading of the roller sleeve. Reload the roller.

TRY IT

Keeping rollers wet

Be prepared for pauses in your work schedule. Have a roll of plastic wrap or a large plastic bag handy. Simply wrap up the roller sleeve to keep the paint roller from drying out while you have your lunch.

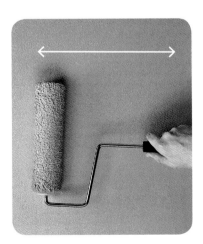

3. Replace the loaded roller onto the previously painted section and distribute the paint using a horizontal backward and forward action. Repeat a few times to unload the roller, then reload to begin finishing off the first section.

4. Place the roller at the top of the section and smooth the paint by lightly drawing the roller vertically from top to bottom. Lift the roller and return it to the top of the section after each stroke. Now begin a fresh section.

TRY IT

Power painting

A power paint roller can speed up the painting process. There is no need to stop and reload your roller every few minutes, as the paint is delivered directly to the roller through a tube from a reservoir of paint.

More painting methods: pads and foam brushes

There are methods of applying paint other than with brushes and rollers – namely paint pads and foam paintbrushes. The paint pad certainly has some benefits, in that the paint coverage is better than with rollers or bristle brushes because the pad applies a very thin film of paint. However, the pad can detach from the handle after prolonged use. Foam brushes are inexpensive and easy to use. They are good for touch-ups, but not for big decorating jobs.

TRY IT

Eliminating paint odors

If you hate how paint smells, cut an onion in half and place it cut-side up in the room. Amazingly, it removes the smell! Strange, but very effective.

TRY IT

Foam paint pads

Paint pads usually come in a kit containing various sizes of pads and a paint-tray loading system. Use the biggest pad for fast coverage for large areas, and a smaller one for cutting in and negotiating obstacles. Some manufacturers supply specialty pads for walls and ceilings that have built-in edging wheels designed to guide the pad precisely along the corner between ceiling and wall.

146   Making the most of foam paintbrushes

Foam paintbrushes are really easy to use. Some decorators find it is easier to control where the paint goes with them, rather than with bristle brushes. One extra advantage is that they do not leave brush marks behind, which is particularly useful when painting moldings. Methods vary, but this is a good one for painting small areas.

1. Decant a small amount of paint into a disposable cup. A cup can be held easily in one hand while you paint with the other. This is useful when you are up a ladder or reaching fiddly areas or tight corners too small for a roller.

2. Dip the tip of the brush into the paint. Do not load the paint beyond the triangular foam tip. As you lift the brush from the paint, twist to collect excess paint and prevent drips.

3. Make gentle strokes on the work surface, lifting the foam brush after each one. Do not press too hard, or the paint will be squeezed out of the foam and form ridges.

Paint pads come in all shapes and sizes suitable for large areas and for cutting in corners.

147   Know when to stop

If a paint job takes more than a day, make sure to stop work when you reach a corner; never stop halfway across a wall or you'll have a noticeable join when you restart the following day.

148 Using a paint pad

Some loading trays included in a paint pad set include a roller, which is designed to load the pad with an even coat every time. This makes for very economical paint use.

1. If you are using an ordinary roller tray to load your pad, pour about ½ in (13 mm) of paint into the reservoir. Dip the pile into the paint and remove any excess by wiping the pad across the ribbed slope.

2. If you have a special tray for the pad, fill it with paint to the depth recommended by the manufacturer. Draw the pad across the roller, which transfers paint from the tray to the pad, then draw it along the back edge of the tray to scrape off excess paint.

3. Start painting by creating a border around the perimeter of the walls at the ceiling. Use a pad with edging wheels or stick short lengths of masking tape on the adjoining surfaces and paint up to them. You can use a small pad to paint around obstacles.

4. For filling in main areas, pull a large pad across the work area in a series of parallel and overlapping passes. Then run the pad across the painted area at right angles to the first passes. Finish off by making light passes, then move on to the next section.

Starting to paint

When you've decided which painting method to employ, you'll need to consider how to start preparing and painting your room. After preparing all the surfaces (see pages 54–61) you'll need to protect all the surfaces you don't want painted, then gather together all of your equipment and paint. Familiarize yourself with the order of work, and then get started.

(see pages 54–61)

TRY IT

Easy ceiling painting

Color-indicator ceiling paint can be very useful when painting ceilings. Horizontal overhead planes can otherwise be very difficult to see clearly. These paints go on pink and then turn white when dry.

149 Painting dos and don'ts

Do:

- Buy testers before committing to a big can of paint.
- Allow plenty of preparation time.
- Mask off floors and woodwork.
- Remove any wall fixtures.
- Gather tools and equipment and make a "tool park" somewhere in the room.
- Use the right tools for the job.
- Buy all your paint at the same time to avoid shade inconsistencies.
- Wear suitable protective clothing.
- Keep leftover paint for touch-ups later.
- Be prepared to apply two coats, perhaps more, to achieve good solid coverage.

Don't:

- Be in a hurry to get finished; mistakes are made that way.
- Paint out of sequence. Stick to the order of work.
- Work in a badly ventilated workspace; your paint won't dry properly and the fumes can be unpleasant.
- Underestimate drying times between paint coats. Allow 24 hours before moving furniture back in.
- Forget to clean your brushes and rollers.
- Replace the paint lid without cleaning the rim.
- Pour waste paint down sinks; always dispose of paint responsibly.
- Apply water-based paint over oil-based finishes, and vice versa. Always use a primer that matches the paint.

150 Ladder safety

Whether you are painting ceiling or walls, you'll need a ladder for areas above your reach. Always make sure the feet of the ladder are steady on the floor and the braces securely locked down before you climb up. When standing on a ladder, always lean toward it. Never extend beyond a comfortable reach as this could cause the ladder to topple over. If you are painting in front of a door that opens inward, be sure to put a note on the other side to warn people.

151 Painting order of work

Always work in a logical fashion, which means starting with the ceiling. Then begin work on the walls, starting in the top right-hand corner of each wall if you are right-handed and vice versa if you are left-handed.

152 Protecting surfaces

Apply a strip of masking tape next to the surface you'll be painting – along door and window frames, for example – unless you have a very steady hand. Protect flooring with a dust sheet.

YOU WILL NEED
- Masking tape
- Dust sheets

1. To protect adjacent surfaces such as wood trim, apply masking tape in short lengths, which are easier to handle and apply than long ones. Firmly press down on the edge next to the surface you are painting to keep paint from seeping underneath it.

2. Tape dust sheets to base boards to keep them from creeping and exposing floorcoverings to splashes. Start with vertical strips to hold the sheet in place, then apply the tape horizontally so paint doesn't drip behind the sheet. Use fabric dust sheets to absorb paint splashes rather than polythene ones.

153 Rollering technique for ceilings and walls

Ceilings are the first and probably the most awkward area you'll tackle. You'll need to use a ladder and paintbrush for cutting in, but the best way to cover large areas is with a roller and extension handle. Walls are next; use the extension handle again to reach tall areas and a hand roller for more accessible parts.

YOU WILL NEED
- Eye protection
- Hair protection
- Paint roller and tray
- Roller extension handle

Ceilings Always use eye protection while painting overhead; hair protection is a good idea too. Attach the extension handle to the roller and begin at the corner farthest from the entry door, working on 3 ft (1 m) square sections. Stand on a ladder or the floor, depending on how high your ceiling is.

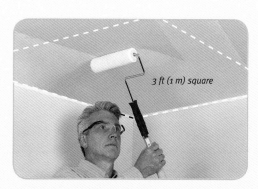

3 ft (1 m) square

Walls Paint walls in 2–4 ft (60–120 cm) sections. Start in an upper corner (1). Then work downward and outward, one section at a time (2). Try not to let a section dry before starting the next.

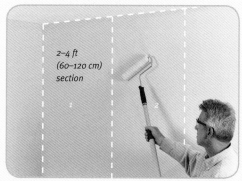

2–4 ft (60–120 cm) section

Brush marks In order to minimize brush marks, slide the roller cover slightly off the roller cage when rolling near wall corners or a ceiling line. Paint applied using a brush or paint pad for "cut-in" areas dries to a different finish than rolled paint.

Paint effects

A well-chosen paint effect can be the answer to some troublesome home-decorating problems. Clever use of paint can be used as a quick fix to disguise uneven wall surfaces or as an instant makeover for furniture; to deceive the eye and create borders and focal points; and to add interest, texture and color whatever your style and without exceeding your budget.

 154   How to achieve a paint effect

The general idea of a paint effect is to combine two or more colors in different ways, either by brushing or sponging one onto another, or by removing part of a topcoat to reveal the base. The method you choose will determine the exact result. Most paint effects use latex paints, and sometimes the colorwash topcoat is combined with a glaze to make it easier to manipulate. You'll need your basic painting kit – brushes, rollers, paint pail, etc. – plus a few extra bits and pieces to make up and apply the glazes required for some finishes.

YOU WILL NEED
- Latex paint for base coats
- Different-colored latex paint for wash
- Water-based glaze
- Natural or synthetic sponges
- Broad floppy paintbrushes
- Clean rags

155   Know your effects

Here are three quick and easy ways to apply color and surface texture to your walls. Colorwashing is a very "loose" style, whereas sponging and ragging require a little more care to avoid pattern repetitions and concentrated areas of color. Make sure to turn your sponge or rag regularly during the painting process so the effect is truly random.

Note: Prepare surfaces thoroughly before applying a paint effect. See pages 54–61.

PAINT EFFECT	APPLICATIONS
Colorwashing	• Method for adding color and the appearance of subtle texture to plain walls; effect can be muted or vibrant depending on the color combination • Useful for disguising surface irregularities
Sponging	• Easily achieved effect using a natural or synthetic sponge • A perfect solution for uneven surfaces • Adds texture and depth
Ragging	• Use to create a more structured finished effect than sponging • Good for plain walls and uneven surfaces

 156   Failsafe colorwash

The easiest way to mix up a topcoat glaze for colorwashing or ragging is to mix one part matte latex paint with four parts water-based glaze. Use a small brush or a stir stick to mix it thoroughly. One and a half pints (1 liter) of colorwash is enough for two coats over an area of 30 sq. ft (3 sq. m).

 157   Roller paint effects

All sorts of decorative textured effects can be produced using a paint roller. Try wrapping elastic bands tightly around the roller sleeve to make irregular striped patterns, or snipping chunks out of a foam roller for a random mottled effect.

158 Easy paint effect: colorwashing

This technique is straightforward to master. Simply paint your wall or ceiling with a plain base coat of matte latex using a brush or roller, and then apply a random wash of a second color glaze over the top.

EXTRAS YOU WILL NEED
- Broad, flexible paintbrush
- Water-based glaze
- Natural or synthetic sponge
- Matte acrylic glaze

1. Using a sponge, colorwash over the base coat using random strokes to cover an area of about 10 sq. ft (1 sq. m). Work all the paint out of the sponge. Allow to dry before applying a second coat. This will build up the depth of color and give a soft, textured look.

2. Use a brush to apply matte acrylic glaze. This will make the wash colors shine through the topcoat and protect the finish. Work the glaze into a small area at a time to ensure an even coverage.

159 Easy paint effect: sponging

The result of using this technique depends on the colors used, the texture of the sponge and the intensity of the sponged pattern. Apply a base coat of matte latex wall or ceiling paint using a brush or roller. Next, sponge on or sponge off a wash of a second latex color over the top (either a natural or synthetic sponge will do).

EXTRAS YOU WILL NEED
- Natural or synthetic sponge
- Water-based glaze if sponging off

1. For sponging on, use latex paint. Simply dilute the latex paint with a little water in a roller tray. Then dip in the sponge and dab it on the wall, aiming to create an even pattern. You can vary the spacing for a more random effect, or use more than one color.

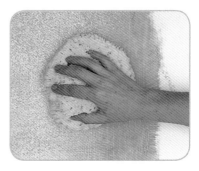

2. For sponging off, use a colorwash glaze. Apply a coat of glaze over the base using a brush, then use the sponge to dab the surface evenly, lifting off some of the glaze each time. Wash the sponge with water when it becomes saturated with glaze, then repeat to create the pattern.

160 Easy paint effect: ragging

This is a similar technique to sponging, but it gives a more structured effect. Apply a matte latex base coat, then a colorwash glaze on top. The idea now is to remove some of the glaze using a crumpled rag, to reveal the base color.

EXTRAS YOU WILL NEED
- Clean lint-free rags
- Water-based glaze
- A helper

1. Apply the colorwash glaze onto the matte base using a large brush. This can be in quite random sweeping strokes. It is best to use a darker wash on top of a lighter base coat. It is also easier to do this as a two-person team – one to wash and one to rag.

2. Crumple a piece of rag and press it firmly onto the wet colorwash in order to lift some of it away from the base coat. Refold the fabric when it is covered with glaze to expose clean fabric. When it is saturated, use a fresh piece. You can wash, dry and reuse the rags for another project.

Taking paint effects further

Paint effects are not just used to create the appearance of surface texture. They can also be used to create stripes, spots, checks, abstract or regular patterns, large-scale images or clever visual tricks. Here are some techniques to use on walls and furniture, and a few ideas for something a little more adventurous.

162   Easy paint effect: distressing

Distressing is a simple technique used to make surfaces look as though they're old and worn. The effect is produced by applying a base coat of a darker shade and a topcoat of a lighter color. A pad of steel wool or fine sandpaper is then used to rub away the topcoat to reveal the darker base. Latex or oil-based paints may be used; the finish can then be protected with a coat of varnish. Here, a small wooden desk, stool and wall paneling have been treated in the same way.

161   What works where

PAINT EFFECT	APPLICATIONS
Distressing	• Useful for creating an aged effect on furniture (tables, chairs, cupboards, kitchen units, wall panels)
Paint patterns	• Simple stripes, different-colored squares, spots or freehand designs can be stunning in the right room
Trompe l'oeil	• If you're really confident with a paintbrush you could try creating the impression of three-dimensional space to "trick the eye" • Can add an illusory dimension to a room
Paint sheen combinations/ Metallic effects	• Perfect for flat walls in the contemporary home • Use in stripes, or geometric and abstract patterns • Use in combination with matte latex paints
Stamping	• Use to achieve an all-over printed wallpaper effect, or a border effect on plain walls
Stenciling	• Borders, geometric patterns, single motifs or words and letters of the alphabet can all be achieved with commercial stencils – or make your own

163 Ideas for paint patterns

- **Stripes** A stunning contemporary effect can be created painting wide horizontal bands of contrasting color. Here the base board has been painted to match the lower stripe.

- **Abstract patterns** Patterns give flair and individuality to a decorative scheme, adding accent colors and interrupting flat expanses of flat color. However, success is a matter of scale; big shapes work well in large rooms but can dominate a smaller area, while small, fussy patterns can get lost in a large room. Try geometric contrasts for a contemporary look. Large random shapes or organic patterns can be simply painted onto a wall freehand or sketched out using a soft pencil first.

- **Metallic effects** Metallic paint finishes can produce startlingly realistic effects of silver, copper, gold and other metals. In natural light metallic paints have a subtle shimmer, but they come to life dramatically under artificial or candle light. Begin with a flat latex base color, then mark off stripes or geometric shapes with masking tape and apply the metallic paint using a roller or brush.

- **Murals** Children love fairy tales! Transform a child's bedroom by creating a mural with characters from their favorite bedtime story or nursery rhyme. It's fun to share the design process with your child, and if the shapes and patterns are simple enough they can help with the painting too. Make sure to use non-toxic, water-based paints and use plenty of drop sheets to protect floor and furniture from spills and fingerprints!

- **Wood-grain effects** This effect is used to imitate the appearance of wood. Why not use pastel shades for a contemporary take on this technique?

- **Stencils** Stenciling is a very simple and inexpensive way to add repeat patterns to a wall and to make a room look unique. Buy ready-made stencils or make your own by cutting out a shape from a large sheet of acetate.

Wallpapering basics

Wallpaper is a popular choice for interior walls and ceilings. The finished effect may be purely decorative, but it can offer practical benefits too: for example, it may be hardwearing and easy to clean, or it may have sufficient thickness and texture to disguise surface imperfections. Wallpapering is not hard, but there are lots of different techniques to learn in order to achieve a good result. Here's what you need to get started.

164 Working out where to start

You'll need a clear idea of where to start. First, make a scale sketch of the room.

- Patterns should be centralized on focal points like chimney breasts. Begin papering here, complete the returns, then paper the alcoves. Now work outward from one corner to complete the room.

- If your pattern is small, or there is no matching required, or the room has no focal points, then simply start at a corner on the largest plain wall and work around the room to complete.

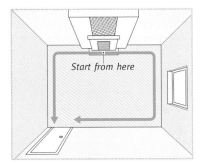

Start from here

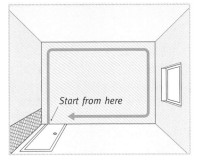

Start from here

165 Centralization: dos and don'ts

Wallpaper with a large or regular pattern will need to be centralized for a balanced effect. The best way to do this is to mark the center of the feature or fireplace, then hold up a dry roll to the wall, matching the center position, and make a pencil mark on the wall at each side. Use a plumb line to mark a vertical as a guide for the first strip.

- **Don't** hang the first length off center; the effect will be unbalanced.

- **Do** centralize the first wallpaper length to balance the pattern.

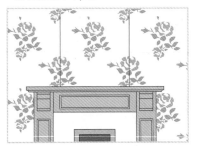

TRY IT

Using pre-pasted papers

Some papers are pre-pasted, so there's no need for a pasting kit. All you need is a shallow water trough, which is filled with water and placed at the base of the wall where the paper is to be hung. However, pre-pasted paper tends to dry out at the edges if you need to cut and shape it around obstacles. Keep a pot of wallpaper adhesive handy so you can paste down the dry edges using a small brush.

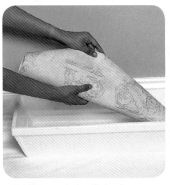

1. Cut the paper to length, leaving a trimming allowance. Roll it with the pattern side and top end outermost. Immerse it in the water trough, and leave it to soak for the suggested time (found on the package).

2. Grip the top edge of the roll and draw it up toward the ceiling.

166 Failsafe cutting and pasting

Before you begin cutting the paper, mix up your wallpaper paste in a large bucket according to directions, and then let it stand. Make sure to mix well to keep lumps from forming. The paste should be usable for about a week.

YOU WILL NEED
- Tape measure
- Wallpaper
- Wallpapering table
- Pencil
- Paper-hanging scissors
- Paste bucket and pasting brush
- Wallpaper paste
- Sponge

TRY IT

Measuring up

After establishing a standard length to which you should cut your paper, subtract the length of your pasting table, then mark that measurement on the table. You can now use the table as a gauge for marking standard lengths of paper. For a pattern repeat, first match the pattern, and then mark it for cutting.

167 Matching batches

When you buy your paper, make sure that the batch numbers are the same on all of the rolls, as colors can vary slightly between batches.

1. Measure the wall height and add 4 in (10 cm) to allow for trimming at the top and bottom. Unroll the wallpaper and mark the length. Fold the paper at the mark, using the edge of the table to make a crease. Write "TOP" on the back of the paper with a pencil as a reminder, and then cut along the fold line.

2. Position the paper on the table so one edge is flush with the far edge of the table. Brush the paste outward to that edge; this ensures that the edges are completely pasted without getting paste on the table, and from there onto the face of the next piece of paper. Use a damp sponge to remove any paste residue from the table immediately.

3. Fold in the pasted end of the length so that the pasted areas are against each other, and slide the length along the table so the remainder can be pasted as described in Step 2. When you have finished pasting the length, fold that end in toward the first.

4. You're now ready to pick up the length and drape it over your arm to carry it to the wall where you intend to hang it. However, if it is heavy paper it will need time to soak; in this case put it aside while you paste another length.

Expert paper hanging

Establishing a true vertical plane is essential when hanging wallpaper, as each strip is guided by the previous one. Never rely on corners as a positioning guide because they are rarely truly vertical. It is usually easier to work clockwise around the room if you are right-handed and counterclockwise if you are left-handed.

TRY IT

Using a plumb line

To ensure that the first strip on each plane lies true to the vertical, use a plumb line. Hammer a small nail into the wall close to the ceiling, then hang the end of the plumb line cord from it, allowing the weight to rest near the base board. Use a pencil to mark at intervals along the string, then draw a straight line between the marks using a pencil and a spirit level.

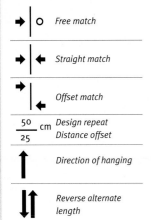

168   Understanding pattern matching

If a number of motifs repeat across a single width of wallpaper, there will be matching halves of the motif at opposite edges – a straight pattern match. If a number of motifs repeat over two widths of paper, the matching halves of the motif opposite edges will be offset by the half pattern repeat – such papers have an offset or drop pattern match. You will find pattern matching symbols on the roll label, which will tell you what kind of pattern your paper has.

PATTERN MATCHING SYMBOLS

➡ ∣ ○	Free match
➡ ∣ ⬅	Straight match
➡ ∣ ⬅	Offset match
$\frac{50}{25}$ cm	Design repeat Distance offset
⬆	Direction of hanging
⬆⬇	Reverse alternate length

Offset or drop pattern match

Straight pattern match

FIX IT

Using lining paper

Use lining paper to smooth out surface imperfections. It provides a smooth surface and even porosity for when you are hanging wallpaper onto less-than-perfect walls. It can also be used on ceilings and can be covered with paint instead of paper. Hang the paper horizontally, with neat butt joints between lengths.

1. After cutting a length of lining paper and pasting it, fold it concertina-fashion to make carrying and hanging it easier.

2. Brush the length out across the wall surface horizontally, fold by fold. Repeat for each subsequent strip.

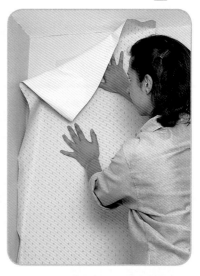

169 Hanging and trimming

You should start wallpapering at a corner of the longest straight wall in the room and take a little time to establish a true vertical plane with the aid of a plumb line. Try to work as quickly as you can because the wallpaper paste can dry out, causing adhesion problems along the seams and joins.

YOU WILL NEED
- Plumb line
- Pencil
- Pasted paper
- Paper-hanging brush
- Paper-hanging scissors
- Sponge

1. If you are starting work in a corner, draw your first plumb line on the wall about 1 in (25 mm) less than the width of the wallpaper from the corner. This allows a small amount of paper to be turned into the internal angle. Hold the line and make two or three pencil marks down the wall to indicate the vertical.

2. Carry your folded length of paper to the wall, climb onto the stepladder and unfold the top end of the length so you can position it against the wall. First slide it upward and allow about 2 in (50 mm) of wallpaper to overlap onto the ceiling, then move it sideways so the edge of the paper lines up with your plumbed line.

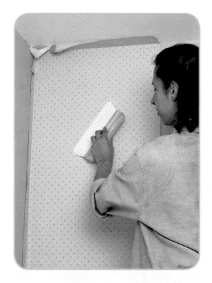

3. Use your paper-hanging brush to smooth the top half of the length onto the wall surface, working from the top downward and from the center toward the edges to brush out any bubbles. Then allow the rest of the length to unfold down the wall and continue to smooth into place. Press the paper well into the corner.

4. Press the back of the blade of your paper-hanging scissors between the wall and ceiling and draw them along to mark the paper. Peel the paper away from the wall and cut along the marked line. Discard the offcut and brush the trimmed end into place. Repeat the process to trim the wallpaper at the base board.

5. Paste and fold the next length of paper, and bring it to the wall. Open the top fold as before, press it against the wall surface and align the pattern with that on the first length. Then brush the length into place and trim top and bottom edges. Wipe away any excess paste using a damp sponge.

Wallpapering around corners and openings

If you are wallpapering a room, you will at some point need to negotiate an internal or external corner (or other projecting features). Room corners are seldom truly square, so if you turn a length of paper from one wall onto the adjacent wall, the edge will no longer appear vertical. Always establish a new vertical on each wall.

FIX IT

Dealing with radiators

If you want to paper behind a radiator, simply tuck about 6 in (15 cm) of wallpaper down behind the top edge of the radiator, and slide the paper behind the side edges as far as you can. A slim paint roller designed to fit behind radiators is ideal for pressing the paper into position. If there is a visible gap between the radiator and the base board, paper that too.

170   Negotiating doors and windows

Papering around these kinds of obstacles is just a matter of careful measuring and trimming, using the same techniques as for internal and external corners.

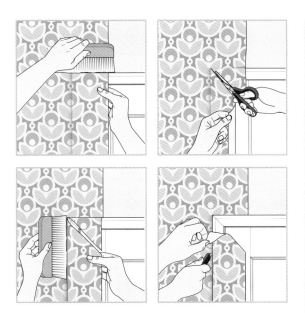

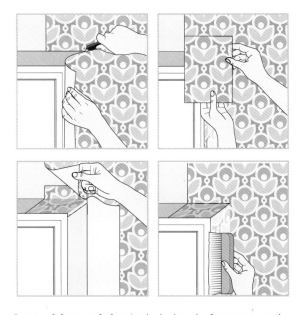

- **Flush door or window** Hang the length next to the door so one edge overlaps the frame, and then make a diagonal cut from the edge into the upper corner of the door/window frame. Crease and trim the paper down the side and across the top of the frame. Then trim neatly. Brush the paper smooth. Hang the next piece above the door/window; cut diagonally into the other corner and repeat the trimming process.

- **Recessed door or window** Apply the length of paper next to the window, allowing it to hang down in front of the recess. Make a horizontal cut just above the top corner, and do likewise at the bottom edge. Fold and smooth the paper into the return. Now cut a small piece of paper to match the width of the overhang. Paste and position it under the overhang, around the foremost external corner and the internal angle at the back. Brush all edges smoothly into place.

171 Papering internal corners ...

Negotiating your way around corners when wallpapering can be a bit tricky, but it is worth getting the technique right as the paper tends to wrinkle if it is not hung correctly.

1. After hanging the last full length before an internal corner, measure the distance from its edge to the internal angle at the top, center and bottom of the wall. Add 1 in (25 mm) to the largest of these measurements, and cut a strip of paper to this width, making sure the cut edge will be next to the corner. (Put aside the trimmed-off piece.)

2. Paste the cut strip and hang it in place, butting the machine-cut edges of the two lengths snugly together. Use your paper-hanging brush to tuck the trimmed edge of the strip well into the internal angle.

3. If the turned edge of the paper creases because the corner is not true, make release cuts in vinyl paper and small tears in standard paper to allow the edge to lie flat.

4. Measure the width of the trimmed-off length that was put aside, and mark a plumb line next to the wall that distance from the corner. Paste and hang the strip with its machine-cut edge aligned with the plumbed line, and brush its hand-cut edge into the internal angle so that it overlaps the turned edge.

172 ... and external corners

It is important that wallpaper on external corners is well adhered. Corners take quite a lot of rough treatment from passing human traffic and can tear if not stuck down properly.

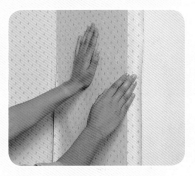

1. At an external corner, use a similar technique to Steps 1 to 3 for internal corners to turn about 1 in (25 mm) of paper around the angle and onto the adjacent wall. Again, make release cuts or tears if necessary to ensure the edge lies flat.

2. Mark a plumbed line on the second wall and hang the leftover length to the line so that its hand-cut edge overlaps the turned section, as in Step 4 of internal corners. If you are hanging vinyl paper, you'll need a special vinyl overlap adhesive.

TRY IT

Neat overlapping

When papering around an external corner, try tearing along the trimmed edge of the underlap. This method is called "feathering," and makes the edge of the underlap less noticeable.

Papering around obstacles and awkward areas

Most walls are interrupted by a number of ill-placed obstacles, light switches and power sockets, and some lead into awkward areas such as stairwells. However, for all papering problems there are solutions; the worst thing that could happen is that your paste dries out while you're measuring and trimming, so make sure you keep a pot of paste and a small touch-up brush at hand.

174   Papering around a light fixture

When papering a ceiling, you will probably come across a light fixture. Simply pierce the paper in the correct position and make lots of radiating scissor cuts from the center. You can now pass the pendant flex through the hole. Unscrew the ceiling rose cover and allow it to drop down the pendant flex, and then continue to apply the rest of the strip. Return to the ceiling rose base plate and trim the tabs neatly. Brush the triangular tabs of paper flat against the ceiling, then screw the cover back into place.

173   A shortcut to avoid

Never attempt to take a lot of paper around a corner as a shortcut. Walls are never perfectly straight or true and you will end up with wrinkles.

TRY IT

Using random designs

If you have a room that is full of awkward shapes and other obstacles, then it may make your job a bit easier to use a wallpaper with a random design. Prominent patterns and large designs can be difficult to match when negotiating lots of corners and recesses.

175   Papering around a light switch

This method also works for power sockets, air vents and any other small obstacles that need papering all the way around. Safety note: Remember to turn off the power supply before loosening face plates of sockets or switches.

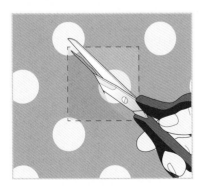

1. Loosen the screws that hold the face plate to its backing box before you start papering. Paper over the face plate, and then press the paper against it to mark the corners. Make a diagonal cut into each corner of the plate, to make four triangular tabs.

2. Trim off all but about ¼ in (6 mm) of each tab. You may find a smaller pair of scissors easier to manipulate here.

3. Tuck the four tabs carefully behind the face plate, and use your paper-hanging brush to ensure that the paper lies flat and bonds well to the wall. Then tighten the fixing screws to trap the tongues in place. Once the paper has been fitted around all the switches and sockets, you can turn the power back on.

176 Accessing ceilings and stairwells

The awkward thing about papering stairwells and ceilings is access. Reaching high walls and working on a horizontal overhead plane is quite tricky, so plan safe access and, ideally, arrange for someone to help. Here scaffolding boards are securely tied to a stepladder and a straight ladder.

Papering a stairwell

Papering a stairwell is a real decorator's challenge. The long lengths of paper required for the side walls are difficult to handle, and access is tricky. Always make sure to tie scaffold boards securely to the steps of the ladder and stepladder before walking on them.

1. Set up a secure access platform, then begin hanging the longest lengths on the side wall. Work up the stairs length by length, trimming carefully at the top and at the diagonal angle at the bottom.

2. It makes sense to cut, paste and trim the upper half yourself, and then ask your helper to do the same with the lower half. Complete the job by finishing the head wall above the foot of the stairs. Then paper the landing as you would a normal room.

Papering a ceiling

The simplest access arrangement for papering a ceiling is a pair of stepladders bridged by two scaffolding planks securely tied together.

1. Nail a string line across the ceiling, about 1 in (25 mm) less than the width of your wallpaper, measured out from the side wall.

2. Paste and fold up the paper strip in a concertina fashion. Position the end of the paper next to the internal angle of the wall and ceiling. A friend is useful here to hold the paper behind you while you position the paper and brush out the wrinkles.

3. When the strip is in place, trim the ends, and make release cuts on the edge that overlaps the side wall in exactly the same way as you would when hanging vertical paper. Repeat the process for subsequent lengths.

String guideline

Fixing wallpaper problems

After a while the appearance of your wallpaper may change. Air bubbles can form under the surface; seams, edges or corners may begin to lift; and everyday traffic may have caused a tear or two. While these mishaps can be annoying, they are easy to fix.

FIX IT

Dealing with air bubbles

Bubbles are formed by trapped air under the paper or by a weak bond between the paper and the wall. There's no need to replace the wallpaper in its entirety unless the problem is widespread over a large area. Feel the bubble first to make sure that it is just air, and there are no pieces of debris under the surface because you will need to remove these before re-pasting.

YOU WILL NEED
- Utility knife or razor blade
- Small brush
- Small adhesive bottle with fine nozzle
- Damp sponge
- Syringe (optional)
- Small foam roller (optional)

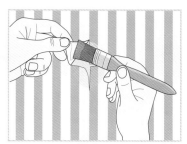

1. Using the utility knife or a razor blade, make two incisions in the shape of an X in the paper over the air bubble. Try to follow the pattern if there is one to make the cut as unobtrusive as possible; you could cut along the edge of a flower or an abstract shape. Gently press on both sides of the cut to release the trapped air.

2. Peel back the tabs or tongues formed by the slits and use a small brush to apply wallpaper adhesive to the back of each one. Gently smooth the tabs back into place using a damp sponge. Squeeze out excess adhesive and wipe it away from the surface or it will form a shiny patch when dry.

3. Alternatively, you could fill a syringe with adhesive to fill the air pocket behind the paper through a smaller slit. Smooth the paper back onto the wall using a small foam roller. Wipe away excess adhesive using a damp sponge.

177   Wallpaper repair tips

- Always keep a few pieces of leftover wallpaper or the odd roll just in case you need to make a repair.

- Some decorating stores sell wallpaper repair kits containing a small roller, adhesive sticks or adhesive in small squeeze bottles for ease of application. Keep one handy just in case.

178   Applying paste

Lots of wallpaper problems occur because the paste has been applied too sparingly, unevenly or has been allowed to dry out before hanging the strip. This results in patches that are poorly adhered to the wall. Try applying the wallpaper paste using a paint roller instead of a pasting brush. Pour the paste into a large shallow bowl or deep tray, and then roll the sleeve in the paste and roller the paste onto the paper. It's quick and easy.

179 How to patch wallpaper

A larger tear can be patched if you have a spare piece of matching paper.
You'll need a utility knife, masking tape and some border adhesive.

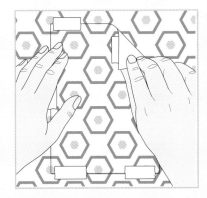

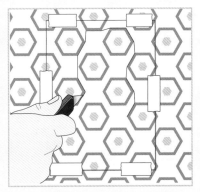

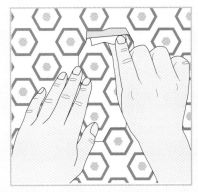

1. Cut a rectangle of wallpaper that is a little larger than the damaged area. Use tabs of masking tape to fix it securely to the wall on all four sides in the correct position, taking care to match the pattern exactly.

2. Now, using a utility knife, carefully cut around the tear though the patch and the paper underneath. If the paper has a pattern, use the design as a guide to the shape of the cut, or if there are stripes or lines use those in order to make the patch as inconspicuous as possible. This will create an exact patch for the damaged area.

3. Remove the rectangle and the patch and dampen the area on the wall to be repaired with warm water in order to soften the adhesive. Carefully peel away the damaged area, apply wallpaper adhesive to the back of the new patch and position it carefully on the wall. Smooth down gently using a damp sponge.

180 Removing stains from wallpaper

- This may seem like an odd way to remove a stain from wallpaper, but it's cheap and effective. You'll need six parts flour, three parts mineral spirits and three parts water. Mix the ingredients, and then knead to form a soft dough. Take a small amount of dough and roll into a ball. Use the ball of dough to rub away the dirty or greasy mark, turning the dough regularly so you always use a fresh surface.

- Remove a greasy stain by rubbing with a small piece of stale white bread, or a soft artist's eraser.

- Grease marks can sometimes be removed with brown paper and a warm iron. Place the paper over the stain then gently press with the iron. The grease will melt and be absorbed by the paper.

- Dry-cleaning fluids can work on wallpaper stains. Spray the product on the stain and let dry, then brush away the resulting powder.

- Always test an inconspicuous area of paper for colorfastness before trying to remove a stain.

TRY IT

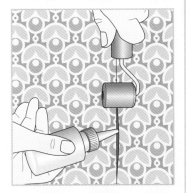

Re-pasting lifted seams

Wallpaper can lift at the seams, and if you don't repair this quickly they can tear, creating a further problem. Lift the loose edge carefully and apply adhesive behind it from a bottle with a fine nozzle. Gently press the seam back into place using a seam roller. Wipe away excess glue using a damp sponge.

FIX IT

Simple wallpaper repairs

- Poorly pasted wallpaper and a moist atmosphere can cause paper to dry out at the lower edge along the base board or in the corners of a room; if not repaired quickly the paper can tear. In this case dampen the lifted area with water, peel back the paper a little farther, then apply border adhesive to the back. Smooth the section back into place using a damp sponge. Fill in gaps along the base board with a bead of filler from a cartridge gun when the adhesive is dry.

- Paper is quite durable but not indestructible. Small tears can often occur, but these are easily fixed. Simply apply adhesive to the back of the tears and smooth gently into position using a damp sponge.

Feature walls

A feature wall is an easy way to create a stunning effect in your home – using a vibrant paint color, an oversized geometric pattern, stripes, textures, wall decals, murals ... anything you fancy, really. The result will draw attention and can showcase a piece of furniture or create a central focal point. A feature wall gives you the chance to try something fun, bold and new without committing to a whole room's worth of paper or paint. Also, it's easy enough to redecorate just one wall if you change your mind or have a different idea in the future.

A very dark color on all four walls can be oppressive. However, one wall in a striking moody shade can create a dramatic effect when teamed with contrast-color accessories or furniture.

TRY IT

Three ways with feature walls

A feature wall, by definition, is a special feature in a room and has to be different from all the other walls. There are three ways to achieve this:

- **Color** A feature wall can be a bold contrast, an intensely dark shade or a bright, vibrant statement of flat color.

- **Pattern** Patterned wallpaper can be used for an almost instant transformation. It won't take long to make a big difference.

- **Texture** This could be in the form of fabric hangings or wallcoverings, floor-to-ceiling bookshelves, beautiful wood panels, exposed brickwork – any treatment that is different in texture from the rest of the room.

181 Feature wall considerations

1. Keep it unique. Don't attempt to use the same feature wall idea in every room; it will lose its impact.

2. Make sure the feature ties in with the rest of the room in some way, otherwise it'll just look out of place.

3. Go for it. It's just one wall. Mistakes can easily be corrected, so let your imagination run wild, and don't be afraid to experiment.

182 Feature paint

- Paint is a nice safe choice for a surface treatment; be bold or be subtle, but always prepare your surface properly first. Flat paint on walls can accentuate poor surfaces (see page 54).

- Color makes the feature. Choose a striking color that complements or matches existing colors or accessories in the room. Bold contrasts need to be tied in with some other elements in the decorating scheme.

- If your feature wall is a strong color, be prepared to apply a few coats to ensure a good solid coverage.

- Wide horizontal or vertical stripes in two complementary colors or simply in black on white can have a dramatic effect on the perception of space. Vertical stripes can make a wall appear taller, while horizontal bands bring the ceiling down to achieve an intimate atmosphere.

- Specialty products like chalkboard or magnetic paint can be used in playful but practical ways in offices, children's rooms, kitchens or utility rooms. Paint large expanses for use as oversized notice boards or calendars.

RIGHT: Decals can add a sense of fun to your decor. They are an easy way of bringing color and interest to a room.

183 Feature wallpaper

- Wallpaper is a classic option for a feature wall. Bold patterns, geometric shapes, wall murals, textures, custom papers; you name it, you can probably buy a wallpaper that features it. It doesn't take a lot of wallpaper to cover one wall, so maybe the budget can stretch to something a little more exotic.

- Oversized bright floral prints can reflect colors and shapes from your own garden if placed near a window or in clear view of a garden.

RIGHT: Here two contrast colors are used to complement a dark, floral chimney breast feature. Traditional furniture adds a quirky touch.

BELOW: Bold oversized floral wallpaper provides a stunning contrast to an otherwise monochromatic bedroom scheme.

184 Fun ideas

- Large vinyl wall decals can transform a room, adding colored shapes, modern graphics, calligraphy, delicate images or fun motifs. They can be bought as a ready-made kit or produced to your specifications.

- Wall-to-wall shelving or a built-in display system creates an impact and draws attention to all your treasures. This is a real statement of who you are.

- Photographs can be blown up and reproduced in a wallpaper format to your specifications. This is a chance to show off your photography skills.

- Metallic wallpaper or mirrors can make a room seem bigger.

- Painting a wall mural yourself or commissioning someone to paint it for you can be a real showstopper.

1. *Using white as a basic background color provides the opportunity to experiment with bold accent colors. A zingy orange dividing wall separates the kitchen from the dining room, which features a block of a more muted, candy pink. Small areas of color are easy to repaint if you change your mind or your accessories.*

2. *Using large wall decals, it's easy to create a woodland in your bedroom! Choose a color that complements or contrasts with other decorative elements you have already.*

3. *Pretty, muted pastels are combined with neutral shades in an oversized repeating peacock pattern in order to provide a focal point that is subtle and fresh, but which retains a contemporary feel. This clever design idea uses several colors at once and goes a step further than simple painted stripes.*

4. *Many home decor companies offer a custom service to transform your photographs into lengths of wallpaper to create a unique interior feature. Simply provide the photograph together with the dimensions of the wall, then all you have to do is paste it into place matching each drop carefully.*

2

5. It is important to consider how color combinations work; subdued natural tones together with a bold pattern repeat produce a striking, yet subtle feature wall. The effect would be different, and possibly overwhelming, if bold patterns and colors were used.

5

Sanding wooden floors

Having tackled painting and decorating on walls and ceilings, you may like to try your hand at the floor too. If you have wooden floorboards that are in good condition, then sanding is an economical alternative to laying down sheet flooring materials. Floor sanding machines and edge sanders are available for rent from hardware stores. The store will also sell safety gear and sanding sheets. Be warned though: this is a noisy and very dusty job.

185 Before you begin

- Clear the room of all items of furniture.

- Wrap pendant light fixtures in clear plastic.

- Remove all floorcoverings.

- Take down all curtains and pictures.

- Thoroughly protect bookcases or audio/electrical equipment with plastic sheets.

- Seal off other rooms to prevent dust migration.

TRY IT

How to "drive" a sander

When the sanding belt has engaged with the floor, don't try to hold it back or keep it in one place as this may cause damage and gouge marks on the wooden surface.

186 Preparing to sand

Take the time to check that all the floorboard fixings are sound and secure. Check too for any squeaky, split or wobbly boards and for protruding nail heads.

YOU WILL NEED
- Nail punch
- Hammer
- Crowbar
- Flooring nails

1. Use a nail punch and a hammer to drive any protruding nail heads below the surface. Place the cupped tip of the punch over each nail head and give a few firm taps with the hammer. Nail heads that jut out will tear the sanding sheet.

2. Wobbly or squeaky boards may be a result of loose nails. Simply re-secure the board using new flooring nails. If dust and debris has collected under the board, between it and the joist below, use a crowbar to lift the board and blow away or vacuum up the debris before you re-secure it.

3. Re-secure loose or split boards by hammering new flooring nails through the board and into the joist underneath. Position the nails either side of the split. Do not reuse old nail holes.

187   How to use sanders

Read the instructions provided with both sanders carefully, and fit sanding sheets as directed. The dust bag will collect most, but not all, of the dust – so keep your vacuum cleaner close by.

YOU WILL NEED
- Face mask/goggles/ear defenders
- Floor sander
- Abrasive sheets
- Vacuum cleaner
- Edge sander
- Sanding block
- Cloth
- Garbage bags for dust collection

Note: Empty the sanding machine's dust bags regularly into an open container, and allow the dust to settle a little before you place the contents in a plastic garbage bag for disposal. Tie up the bags securely to keep the dust from escaping.

1. Put on your safety gear. Position the floor sander on the boards starting in one corner, and begin sanding with overlapping diagonal sweeps across the boards, using coarse abrasive sheets. Go over each section several times, and then sand again across the other diagonal.

2. Vacuum up any remaining dust. Fit medium-grade abrasive sheets to the sander, then re-sand the floor, this time working along the line of the floorboards. If you're sanding a herringbone block floor, follow the diagonal lines.

188   Save your ears

Sanding is a noisy process, so always wear ear defenders. It's dusty too, so a face mask is essential. Tell your neighbors in advance that you will be making noise; sand in daylight hours only to prevent too much disturbance.

3. Go around the edge of the room using a handheld edge sander. Move the sander in a circular motion, allowing it to overlap the previously sanded areas. Start with a medium-grade abrasive paper, then change to a finer grade.

4. You'll need to sand into the corners using a sanding block wrapped in abrasive paper. Finally, sweep up all the dust and vacuum thoroughly. Wipe the entire floor with a damp cloth to remove any dust particles that may spoil the subsequent decorative treatment.

Decorative treatments for wooden floors

When the floorboards have been sanded, vacuumed and wiped clean and all the dust disposed of, you can begin to think about a decorative treatment. A starting point would be to decide if you want to still see the wood grain after you have applied the finish – or not. Use a varnish or stain if you do, and use a floor paint if you don't.

189 Fabulous floor finishes

- **Varnish** This enhances the natural wood grain and leaves a transparent protective coat. Varnish is available in clear form or various wood tones.

- **Wood stain** This is similar to varnish but can be tinted with color. The grain will still be visible beneath a colored protective layer. If a deeper color is required, several coats may be applied. Stained floors must be varnished afterward.

- **Paint** Floor paint is very durable and gives excellent coverage. Use this treatment to add a solid color to your boards, and to disguise replacement boards.

190 Floorboard effects: painting

Floor paint is easy to apply and is very durable. It can also be touched up and repainted when signs of wear and tear appear.

YOU WILL NEED
- Steel wool
- Mineral spirits
- Masking tape
- Rubber gloves
- Primer
- Large paintbrush
- Paint roller with extension handle
- Floor paint
- Smaller paintbrush
- Paint roller
- Matte-finish sealer
- Paint pad
- Fine-grade abrasive paper
- Lint-free cloth

1. Clean the floor with a pad of steel wool soaked in mineral spirits to remove any dirt or greasy residue, and let it dry. Protect the base boards by applying a strip of decorator's masking tape along the lower edges. Wear rubber gloves.

2. Mix the primer well, then use a 4 in (10 cm) wide paintbrush to apply the primer around the perimeter of the room next to the base boards. Now paint the remainder of the room using a paint roller fitted with an extension handle. Let the primer dry.

191 Where to begin

Always begin at the edge of the farthest wall and work toward the entry door – don't paint yourself into a corner.

3. Using floor paint, cut in along the base boards with a paintbrush, then paint the remainder using a paint roller. Always roll from a dry area to a wet area to minimize lap lines. Wait for this coat to dry before applying a second coat.

4. When the paint is dry, apply two or three coats of a matte-finish, water-based polyurethane sealer, using a paint pad attachment on the extension pole. Allow the sealer to dry. Sand lightly using a fine-grade abrasive paper, then wipe off dust using a damp lint-free cloth.

192 Floorboard effects: varnishing and staining

Natural wood floors can be transformed and protected with stains and varnishes. The best effects will be achieved on new or newly sanded floorboards. Stains are available as water-based or oil-based versions, but these should not be used together.

YOU WILL NEED
- Steel wool
- Mineral spirits
- Rubber gloves
- Floor stain or varnish
- Lint-free cloth
- Large paintbrush
- Fine-grade abrasive paper
- Sanding block

1. Before you apply any decorative finish, the floorboards must be cleaned with a pad of steel wool soaked in mineral spirits to remove any dirt or greasy residue. Let dry, then proceed with the application; wear rubber gloves.

2. If using a stain, mix it up as directed in a paint pail and apply using a soft lint-free cloth. Work quickly along the length of a few boards at a time so the stain does not dry out in the middle of a length.

3. If using a varnish, apply using a brush and work along each board in turn. You must allow adequate drying time between coats, and be prepared to apply several coats. Each coat will result in a deeper color.

4. After the first coat of varnish dries, lightly rub the surface with fine-grade abrasive paper wrapped around a sanding block. Work with the grain to avoid making scratches. This creates a key for the subsequent coats of varnish. Wipe away any dust particles with a cloth before applying the next coat.

Cleaning up

Cleaning up is probably the job that every home decorator dreads! How you go about it and what cleaning products you use will depend on the kind of paint you've used. If you've bought an inexpensive decorating kit, then you may be tempted to discard it and buy a new one for the next time. However, if your brushes and rollers were expensive then it makes sense to clean and store them carefully. Good equipment can last a long time if it is looked after properly; follow these tips to make cleaning up less of a chore.

TRY IT

Avoiding dried-up paint

If you need to stop halfway through a painting job, simply place your brush or roller into a plastic bag or plastic wrap. This ensures that the paint stays wet and ready to use after your break.

193   Which cleaner?

CLEANING PRODUCT	TYPE OF PAINT/CLEANING METHOD
Solvents – brush cleaner or mineral spirits	**Alkyd/oil-based paint** When the paint job is finished, work the paint out of the brush onto a sheet of newspaper. Then immerse the bristles in mineral spirits and flex them. Blot on some paper towel, and then wash with soapy water. Rinse and let dry. Solvents aren't pleasant to use and can irritate the skin, so wear protective gloves and use in a well-ventilated area.
Water and detergent	**Latex/water-based paint** As soon as you finish painting, wash the brushes/rollers in warm soapy water, rinse with clean water and let dry. Flex the bristles between your fingers to work the paint residue out of the roots.

FIX IT

Rescue your paintbrush

If, after a long hard day of painting, you forget to clean your best paintbrush, do not despair. Hardened paint can be removed using this simple method. Drill a hole through the handle, just above the ferrule, then insert a large nail. Fill a glass jar with mineral spirits or brush cleaner, and suspend the brush in the jar as shown. Leave overnight, then wash out with detergent and warm water. Do not simply stand the brush in the jar, as the bristles may become distorted.

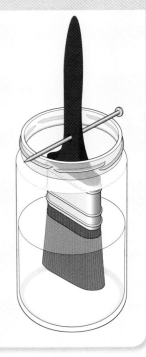

194   Cleaning paint cans

It's not just about brushes and rollers; don't forget to clean the paint cans! Always clean the rims before replacing the lids, and wipe up any drips on the outside of the can. Use a waterproof marker to indicate the level of the paint on the outside of the tin. Saves opening it up to see how much is left if you need it for touch-ups.

TRY IT

Storing pads and rollers

Always wrap dry rollers in a plastic bag to protect them from dust. Then stand them on end if possible to avoid crushing the pile and creating a flat spot. When storing paint pads, try not to rest the pad on anything that could make a dent or flat spot on the sponge.

195 How to clean a paint roller

This can be a time-consuming process. Scrape the excess paint from the roller cover using the curved side of a cleaning tool – you can also use the back of a knife or a large spoon. Wash the roller cover with warm water and detergent, then rinse clean under a running tap. Let dry completely before storing.

Cleaning tool

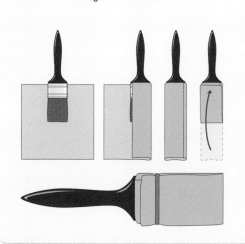

196 How to clean a paint pad

Paint pads are easy to clean because the sponge pad is quite thin and does not retain a lot of paint residue. Hold the pad under running water, and then squeeze out the paint residue with your fingers. Press the pad against the side of the sink to remove the water. Let it dry before storing.

197 Caring for your kit

- **Roller trays and paint pails** If possible, try to scrape away excess paint, and replace it in the paint can if it's not too contaminated with dry paint flakes or dirt. Wash with warm soapy water, rinse and let dry.

- **Dust sheet** A good dust sheet will last years. When you have finished your decorating, take the sheet outside and shake out all the loose bits of dust, paint and debris. Refold neatly and store in a plastic bag for future projects.

- **Wallpapering table** Wash away paste residue when you have finished; dried paste or paint will be lumpy and will spoil your wallpaper next time.

- **Tiling tools** Grout and adhesive are difficult to remove when dried, so scrape residue off tools, rinse with warm water and detergent and then dry before storing.

198 Removing paint drips

- Stray latex paint drips can be cleaned from woodwork using a damp cloth if the paint is still wet.

- Dry spots of paint on woodwork can be flicked or picked off very carefully using your fingernails.

- Dried paint on window glass can be gently scraped away using a flexible scraper or the blade of a utility knife.

- Wet paint on clothes can be removed with soapy water if latex, and mineral spirits if alkyd. If it has dried on then try dry-cleaning fluid, or as a last resort just keep those clothes for painting, as the paint is there to stay.

199 Do it now!

Remember to clean brushes and rollers before the paint dries – it's so much easier!

4

Doors, windows and finishing touches

Doors, windows and other decorative and functional features may not be the first thing you think about as a home decorator, but they do form a vital part of the overall scheme. They have a significant visual impact and therefore deserve the same careful attention as walls and ceilings. This chapter examines the surfaces you're likely to encounter and how to repair, prepare and decorate them with ease. There are also hints and tips on finishing touches, from decorative trims to functional hardware and home security.

Surface considerations

Windows and doors can be made from a variety of different materials – typically wood – but metal or uPVC are also used. There are advantages and disadvantages with all materials, and there are different decorating decisions to make depending on what you have in your home. If the budget is tight you will not be able to replace windows and doors, but you will need to make do and mend them instead.

200 Window materials at a glance

MATERIAL	CHARACTERISTICS	CONSIDERATIONS
Wood	• A porous natural material used for window and door construction. • Wood constructions tend to react to seasonal changes and can swell, contract and warp.	• Requires regular maintenance and repainting. • The advantage of wood is that it will accept any paint finish you like; stain or varnish or apply a color to suit your decor. Simply sand or strip to prepare, and paint using alkyd or water-based products.
Metal	• Metal window and door frames don't swell or contract due to seasonal changes in humidity like wood does. • They can be prone to rust.	• Metal frames are tough and durable, but require the use of specialized paint suitable for metal surfaces. • Chemical paint stripper is recommended, as a heat gun may cause the glazing to crack.
uPVC	• Vinyl windows can offer the home decorator several advantages, in that they are relatively maintenance free. • They don't expand or contract like wood, and the finish doesn't chip or peel like paint. • Vinyl can discolor over time.	• Special vinyl cleaner or white vinegar solution can be used to freshen up old, tired windows and doors. • Frames can also be painted using acrylic paint products.

201 Wait for ideal conditions

When painting exterior windows and doors try to do so on a calm, still day. Wind can blow fine airborne dust and grit, which can stick to the surface of a fresh coat of paint. Small dust particles are sometimes hard to spot until the paint is dry, and then you have to sand the surface and start all over again!

FIX IT

Cleaning and painting uPVC

In general, vinyl windows and doors will not require much maintenance, but if yours are old they may need a bit of attention. Here's how to renovate them. (Note: Vinyl (uPVC) windows tend to degrade toward the end of their lifespan, and renovation is always a temporary fix. Replacement will be necessary at some point.)

1. **Clean** – Mix three parts distilled white vinegar to seven parts water and pour into a spray bottle. Spray the solution onto the surface, allow to stand for a few minutes, reapply the spray solution and then use a soft brush to clean and brighten the frames. Wipe down with a damp cloth. Do not use bleach, acetone or abrasive cleaners on vinyl surfaces.

2. **Paint** – Clean surfaces and use a fine-grade abrasive paper to create a key. Now tape off any glazed sections. Make sure there are no dust particles before applying a thin coat of acrylic primer with a small brush. Try to work quickly, as any dust that settles on the paint surface will spoil the finish. Apply the topcoat when the primer is dry.

TRY IT

Preparing metal for painting

You may need to strip metal surfaces. Here's how to do it:

- Use paint-stripper gel. Simply brush it on, and once the paint has softened, scrape it off with a scraper or shave hook. Kitchen scourers and a small wire brush can help to dislodge stubborn paint residue. Wash down the surface with soapy water when stripping is complete.

- Use abrasive paper to smooth off any surface imperfections, and apply a coat of rust inhibitor if necessary.

- Safety note: Paint-stripping products are highly caustic and will burn skin and damage eyes. Always wear protective goggles and gloves.

202 Spray painting vinyl windows

Spray paint can be useful for vinyl windows and doors, as it provides even coverage without brush marks. However, you must mask off everything you don't want painted, as the paint spray will migrate and other surfaces can be contaminated by paint "fallout."

203 A few points about windows and doors

Most homeowners have a budget to adhere to and will work with existing doors and windows, rather than replacing them. However, simple internal replacement doors and small windows can be inexpensive.

- **New wooden doors** Generally these arrive unfinished, so you will need to prime them before painting. Always choose a style to match the current decor. A door is quite a large surface so it provides an excellent opportunity to add a splash of color.

- **Classic wood-paneled internal door** The wood can be repainted to match a new color scheme or stripped, rubbed down and stained or varnished to enhance the natural beauty of the wood grain.

- **Wooden windows** These can be treated in exactly the same way as doors or decorative trims. Simply rub down and repaint, or strip down then apply a paint color or finish of your choice. Windows are an awkward job so make sure to allow plenty of time for them.

- **Vinyl windows** These are the ideal choice for a basement or any other room likely to have a damp or moist atmosphere. Vinyl does not react to seasonal changes so it will not rust, expand or contract.

204 How to paint a radiator

Wall-mounted fittings are easy enough to move and replace when decorating, but a radiator is better left in situ. You can use small long-handled rollers to paint the walls behind a radiator. Then use the same technique to refinish the radiator itself. Choose a color to match the wall, or go for a contrast.

YOU WILL NEED

- Dust sheet
- Scrubbing brush
- Bucket
- Mild detergent
- Wire brush
- Abrasive paper or sanding sponge
- Damp cloth
- Cutting-in brush
- Bendable paint pad

Note: If you suspect the paint job to be pre-1979, it may contain lead, which is dangerous. Use a lead-testing kit, following the manufacturer's instructions. If the test is positive, you'll need to consult a specialist; otherwise proceed as follows.

1. Put down a dust sheet, and wash the radiator using a scrubbing brush and a mild detergent. Rinse off any suds with clean water. Let it dry completely. Brush all surfaces using a wire brush to remove loose paint flakes.

2. Sand the surfaces of the radiator using a folded sheet of abrasive paper or a flexible sanding sponge, paying extra attention to areas where the old paint is cracking or peeling. Wipe the surface with a damp cloth to remove dust.

3. Turn on the radiator until the surface is slightly warm. Apply the paint with a narrow cutting-in brush using long, smooth strokes. Use a bendable painting sponge to access awkward areas and the back of the fins.

TRY IT

Using spray paint

Heat-resistant paint comes in spray form and is easy to use. Always apply two coats for the best coverage. Hold the can about 12 in (30 cm) away from the surface, clearing the nozzle regularly. Make sure to cover the walls and surrounding floor area with a plastic sheet to protect it from paint "fallout."

205 Choosing a look

Before you repaint a radiator, consider the color. Is it a beautiful vintage piece that can stand out as a unique feature? If it is a modern style that would be better being less obtrusive, you can paint the radiator the same color as the wall to blend it into the rest of the room.

Repairs to doors and windows

Windows, doors and trim often require minor repairs before you can begin the paint job. Modern plastic and metal windows and doors are invariably double glazed and require very little maintenance; wooden framework, however, may need a little more attention from time to time. Here are a few fixes for some common window and door problems.

206 Quick fixes for doors and windows

- Too much paint on the closing edges can cause a door to stick. Strip off the paint and apply a thinner coat.

- Windows may bind in the frames due to a paint buildup; in this case simply rub down or strip.

- If your sash window doesn't slide smoothly, rub a candle on the sides of the frame and along the surfaces of the guide beading.

- A door may swell in damp weather and bind in the frame; first establish where the binding occurs then sand or plane it smooth to achieve a better fit.

- Loose hinges can cause a door to bind at the bottom – in this case you can tighten the screws or insert larger screws.

- Creaky door hinges? Simply apply a drop or two of light lubricating oil.

FIX IT

Quick fixes for windows

Do your sash windows work? Previous occupants may have applied several coats of paint to the windows, sticking them together. Paint can seep between the jamb and the sash, creating quite a firm bond. Don't be tempted to simply paint over it – fix it first.

1. Run the blade of a sharp utility knife between the jamb and the sash to slice through the paint layer. Proceed with caution, grip the knife firmly and move slowly; too much haste can cause the knife to slip, making deep scratches in the surrounding woodwork.

2. If paint has seeped behind the sash, it will be necessary to apply a little more force. Use a wide-bladed scraper and a narrower filling knife, the former to protect the jamb and the latter as a lever to free the sash. Insert the blades as shown, and gently lever the sash free.

TRY IT

Mending door joints

Most wooden windows and doors have mortise and tenon joints, which can shrink as the wood dries out and cause the window or door to sag or bind in the frame. You can easily remedy this by drilling a hole through the joint, passing through both the mortise and the tenon, using a dowel-cutting drill bit; insert dowels smeared with wood adhesive, clamp the joint firmly and then let dry. Chisel off the excess dowel on both sides. Then sand smooth. You can do this in situ, but you may have to remove the door/window from its frame.

TRY IT

Release a stuck window

A paint zipper is a useful gadget used for freeing stuck windows. Serrated edges on the blade saw through layers of old paint and dirt trapped between the sash and the window jamb. The sharp-pointed tip can be use for gaining access to tight corners and scraping paint from window fittings.

207 Common door problems

It's worth fixing all those annoying little problems before you begin to apply decorative finishes to doors.

• **Repairing a loose hinge** If the screws of a hinge are loose, take them out then re-drill each hole the diameter and depth of small lengths of dowel. Apply wood adhesive to the dowel, and then tap into each hole. When the adhesive is dry, drill a pilot hole into each dowel to take new screws for the hinge.

• **Fixing a rattling door** If the door rattles in its frame, reposition the striker plate of the door latch. Unscrew the plate and use a chisel to enlarge the width of the recess on the side closest to the door stop. Drill out the screw holes and glue in dowels; after the adhesive dries, drill new pilot holes and screw in the plate.

• **Replacing damaged wood** Remove the damaged wood using a chisel and a hammer. Cut a small piece of timber, and use abrasive paper to create a good fit for the cutout area. Add wood adhesive to the fixing piece and push it into the hole. Fill any gaps with wood filler when dry, and sand smooth.

208 Dealing with rot

Wet rot softens the wood and usually attacks windowsills and the lowest frame member (rail) of softwood frames, where moisture can collect. If the damage is serious the only solution is to replace the frame; however, you can repair small areas of damage yourself by using a wet rot kit. The kit consists of a wood hardener and a filler.

Note: Dry rot requires an expert fix.

YOU WILL NEED
• Bradawl
• Chisel
• Heat gun
• Wet rot kit
• Brush
• Filling knife
• Sanding block

1. Determine the extent of the rot by poking it with the point of the bradawl – rotten wood will be soft and spongy. Remove the affected areas with a chisel. Use a heat gun to dry the wood if it is still damp. Now brush on the wood hardener from the wet rot kit, and let dry. Apply a second coat if necessary.

2. Mix together the resin-based wood filler and hardener provided in the kit; apply using a filling knife, leaving it to protrude a little from the surrounding surface. If you need to apply more than one layer, let the first one dry before applying the second. When it has dried, sand it flush with the surrounding surfaces.

209 Replacing a window pane

It isn't difficult to replace a pane of glass, but you must take great care to avoid injury when handling broken glass. Glass suppliers can cut the glass to the exact size you want. When you take measurements for the new pane, make sure to allow a ⅛ in (3 mm) clearance on all sides.

YOU WILL NEED
- Dust sheet
- Safety goggles
- Protective gloves
- Chisel
- Pincers or pliers
- Paintbrush
- Wood primer
- Tape measure
- Glass cut to size
- Putty
- Filling knife
- Matchsticks
- Glazing tacks
- Pin hammer

FIX IT

Putty problems?

If putty contains too much linseed oil, it can stick to your hands and be difficult to use. The answer is to roll it around on newspaper, which will absorb the excess oil until the putty is the correct consistency. If the putty has dried out, make it more pliable by adding linseed oil. Clean putty residue off glass surfaces with mineral spirits.

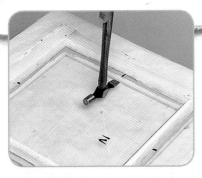

1. Place a dust sheet over your work then while wearing goggles and protective gloves, remove any loose shards of glass. Chisel out the old putty from the rabbet. Remove old glazing tacks using pincers or pliers. Apply a coat of wood primer to the clean rabbets, and let dry.

2. Check that the new pane is the correct size. Knead a ball of putty in your hands until it is pliable; run a bead ⅛–¼ in (3–5 mm) around the bottom of the rabbets. Use a filling knife to press the bead flat and to smooth it out. Trim off any excess putty that may hang over the edge.

3. Insert the glass into the frame. Gently press it into place, leaving an equal gap all the way around. Always press around the edge and never in the middle of the pane. If the window is in situ, you will need to use a few matchsticks along the bottom edge to keep the pane in place.

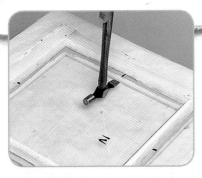

4. Use glazing tacks to secure the glass in place. Slide the flat end of the pin hammer backward and forward across the surface of the glass to lightly tap the tack into place. Do not tap the tack as you would a nail because you may break the glass.

5. Knead and roll the putty into a long, thin sausage shape. Starting at one corner, lay the putty down, pushing it against the sides of the rabbets in the frame. Continue moving the putty along all four sides of the frame.

6. To make a smooth bevel in the putty, hold a putty knife at a 45-degree angle with its straight edge on the putty and pull it along. To miter each corner, place the knife diagonally in the center and pull away from the corner. Allow the putty to dry for at least a week before painting.

Surface preparation: doors

The first thing you'll need to do when painting a door is remove all the door furniture: door handles, escutcheons or finger plates. Always keep any fixing screws together in a plastic bag for reassembly later. If the existing paint job is in good condition, you can rub it down and apply the new paint. If it has been poorly painted or is flaking or damaged, you'll need to strip it and start again.

210 How to use chemical stripper

Although chemical strippers are not economical for large areas, they are ideal for moldings and intricate surface details. Chemical strippers come either in gel or liquid form and are applied with a brush. Heavily layered paint may require more than one application.

YOU WILL NEED
- Dust sheet/newspaper
- Protective gloves
- Chemical stripper
- Glass jar
- Paintbrush
- Scraper
- Shave hook
- Sponge
- Mineral spirits

1. Cover floor areas with a dust sheet or several layers of newspaper before you begin. Wearing protective gloves, decant the stripping solution into a glass jar. Apply a thick layer to the painted surface, working from the top downward. Leave in place in accordance with the manufacturer's instructions.

2. When the paint has softened, use a wide-bladed scraper on the flat areas of the wood and a shave hook on moldings to remove paint, taking care not to gouge the surface of the wood. When the paint has been removed, wipe down the area with a sponge soaked in mineral spirits.

211 Heat stripper tips

- You can use a heat gun prior to using chemical stripping solutions, but it is dangerous to use it afterward; the chemical residue could become vaporized and ignite.

- Avoid using a heat gun in a draft, as the air flow may dissipate the heat before it softens the paint. Also, the melted paint is hot, so try not to drop any on your feet as you work.

TRY IT

Using a heat shield

Using a heat gun to strip paint is useful when stripping off multiple layers quickly and easily; however, the heat can damage surrounding surfaces unless you use a heat shield. Use a piece of sheet metal or simply wrap a thick piece of cardboard with heavy-duty aluminum foil. The guard may be held in position with tabs of decorator's tape.

212 How to heat strip paint

If old paint is heavily layered or badly applied or chipped, it should be completely stripped before repainting. Using a heat gun encourages the paint to blister and pull away from the wood so you can easily scrape it away with a flat-bladed knife.

YOU WILL NEED

- Heat gun
- Brush or paint scraper
- Safety goggles
- Old can or other heatproof container
- Shave hook

213 Schedule in breaks

A heat gun emits a constant flow of very hot air. Make sure to allow for plenty of breaks in your work schedule, in order to avoid overheating the gun and clogging the air with paint fumes.

214 Stripping fine moldings

When stripping paint from fine moldings, it can be difficult to get paint residue from small crevices. Instead of scraping too hard with a shave hook and possibly causing damage to the wood, use a toothpick or a long, thin shard of wood.

1. A heat gun looks rather like a hairdryer, but it emits a powerful heat. You must take care not to scorch the wood; if the paint looks gummy, it may be overheating. To begin, brush or scrape away any loose flakes of paint.

2. Wearing safety goggles, hold the heat gun about 2 in (5 cm) away from the surface. Starting on the lowest setting if the gun is adjustable, move it in a circular motion until the paint begins to blister. If this is not successful turn the heat up to the next setting.

3. Follow the heat gun with a metal scraper. Hold the scraper at around a 30-degree angle, moving both the scraper and the gun at the same speed. Strip all the large flat areas first, depositing all the ribbons of paint in an old can or any other heatproof container.

4. Heat strip the contoured and uneven areas using a shave hook in order to remove the loosened paint. Do not overheat the paint or use too much pressure around detailed areas, as they are more vulnerable to scorching and gouging than flat planes.

10 Points for preparation

Make sure to schedule in plenty of time for window preparation; it can be laborious and tiring so it's best to split it into several work sessions, depending on how many windows you have to prepare. Work through these 10 steps methodically; it really will pay off in the end.

1 Hardware Remove all locks, closures and other fixings because they will interfere with smooth sanding processes. Fill fixing holes if replacing with new hardware.

2 Wash Wash away grease, dirt and grime with a sponge and a sugar soap (or trisodium phosphate) solution. Don't soak the wood, rinse often and work from top to bottom.

3 Sand Sanding by hand is probably the best way to prepare window surfaces – it's hard work and time-consuming, but it's worth it. Flexible sanding sponges are great for this.

4 Scrape If your paint is flaking and chipped you'll need a bit more than sanding to make a good surface; in this case use a carbide blade scraper. It rakes away loose paint without gouging.

5 Stains Apply knotting compound to knots exposed by sanding or scraping. Knots can release resins that will stain new paint topcoats.

6 Crevices Use the point of a putty knife or paint scraper to ease paint from tight crevices and corners.

7 Fill Use a shrink-resistant filling compound to repair surface imperfections. Let dry and sand smooth before painting.

8 Rebuild Damaged wood trim can be repaired and built back into shape by using a two-part filling compound. Simply apply to the damaged area, and shape it roughly to match the trim. Sand the repair smooth when dry.

9 Fill cracks Repair cracks and gape between the frame and the wall using a filling gun.

10 Vacuum After sanding and wiping down, wait a little while for any dust to settle, and then vacuum up all loose, flaked dust particles as they will spoil your new paint finish.

Surface preparation: windows

The home decorator's mantra should be "preparation pays." A successful paint job on a window relies on careful preparation beforehand; window surfaces are similar to door surfaces, but the big difference is that there are lots of complicated moldings to consider. Make sure you have the necessary know-how to make your job easier.

Time-saving sanding

- If you have lots of windows and, therefore, lots of awkward areas to sand, investing in a good-quality detail sander would be a good idea. Sanding is always hard work, so having a little power behind your elbow will help.

- Paint de-glossing products are a liquid form of sanding. They act as a fine abrasive and are used to prepare surfaces for finishing and to remove grease, dirt and wax. Simply wipe the surface with the de-glossing liquid to ensure a good bond. This is useful to replace standard sanding techniques if you have a gloss finish or lead-based paint as a base.

Note: De-glossing products can only be used if the original paint surface is sound.

215 Concealing filler

Remember to apply primer to filled areas when refinishing previously painted wood. The repair may be very smooth and unobtrusive, but unless primed, the filler will show through as a dull spot and spoil the new paint finish. Sand smooth when dry.

217 Fixes for window surfaces

There's no point repainting a window if there are gaps and cracks around the frame or if the moldings have come adrift. You will need to fix it first.

- Use a general-purpose filler cartridge with a filling gun. The pointed nozzle is ideal for filling cracks where the frame has come away from the wall.

- Check for loose moldings, and use wood glue to secure them in position.

- Fill holes and other imperfections with wood filler, and sand smooth when dry.

216 Top tape tips

Masking tape or decorator's tape can be a lifesaver if your hands are shaky and you want a nice clean edge between paint and window pane. However, cheap masking tape can leave sticky residue on glass and can also dry out and deteriorate after prolonged exposure to the air. Buy good-quality tape, and keep it in a plastic bag in your toolbox.

218 How to tell if your paint job is good

It's tempting to repaint over old paint to reduce preparation time, but you should only do this if the previous paint job is good. Using a utility knife, lightly score an X into the old surface, then press a tab of duct tape onto it. Rip off the tab to see if the paint comes off too – if it does, you need to strip it off; if it doesn't, you can give it a light sand and repaint.

219 Three surfaces you may encounter

"Can I paint over it?" The answer to this question is generally "yes." However, the condition the surface is in will affect how much effort will be required to prepare it well enough for priming and painting.

- **Minimum effort** New surfaces – but even brand-new wooden surfaces need a little attention before priming and painting them. Sand lightly with a fine-grade abrasive paper, and then wipe away all traces of dust with a damp cloth.

- **Moderate effort** Sound painted surfaces – you do not need to rub down to the wood if the paint layer is sound. First wash with a sugar soap (or trisodium phosphate) and water solution. Then sand to remove the previous surface paint finish, especially if it is a high-gloss paint.

- **Maximum effort** Poorly painted surfaces – a really bad paint job should be stripped right back to the bare surface; otherwise, scrape away loose flakes and rub down until smooth. Touch up bare areas with primer.

Smart sanding

- Windows have lots of corners and narrow areas, so sometimes it's just not possible to use an electric sander, unless it has a small detail sanding pad.

- Use clog-resistant abrasive paper or pads, as you'll have lots of intricate surfaces to deal with. Ordinary abrasives tend to fill up with particles.

- A sanding sponge works really well for molded areas, as it's flexible and can reach into awkward crevices and curves.

- Fold a piece of abrasive paper, and use the fold to sand into corners.

- Use a piece of abrasive paper and a sanding block for flat areas around the frame or the windowsill.

Paint processes and systems: doors

Doors receive quite a lot of wear and tear, so they need to be protected by a coat or two of a tough hardwearing paint, either alkyd or water-based. The design of your door can vary from a plain flush style to a multipaneled type that requires a bit more thought when it comes to painting. In order to achieve a good result you'll need to follow a logical system of paint application.

220 System for painting a paneled door

This type of door can be tricky to paint successfully because of the many different planes created by the panels and moldings. Follow this order of work to avoid overpainting and accumulation of paint in the edges and corners of the decorative molding. Cover the floor with a dust sheet before you begin.

1. Use a 1 in (12 mm) brush to paint the panel moldings.

2. Paint all four panels in turn, taking care not to allow paint to build up in the corners.

3. Apply paint to the top, center and bottom rails.

4. Paint both center vertical sections – known as "muntins" – which are situated between the pairs of panels.

5. Next paint the two outermost vertical sections, called "stiles," using long, light, vertical paint strokes.

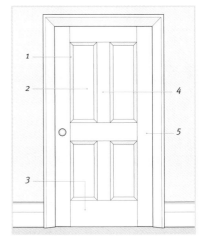

YOU WILL NEED
- Dust sheet
- Paintbrushes
- Paint

221 Tips for a perfect finish

- Always paint with the grain of the wood.
- Try to finish a complete door in one session, as the joins will be noticeable if you stop and restart when the previous paint is dry.
- If the door is a different color on either side, always paint the latch edge to match the face that will open into the room. Paint the hinge edge to match the other face.

TRY IT

Unstick your door

When you paint interior doors there is a tendency for the door to stick a little in the frame when closed again. Wait for the paint to dry completely, then rub a candle along the edges where they make contact with the frame. The wax residue will prevent sticking.

222 System for painting a flush door

A flush door is an easier painting task to handle than a paneled door, but there is still a system for making sure your paint finish is perfect.

1. Imagine that the flush face of your door is divided into eight equal sections.

2. Begin at the top left-hand corner and work across and downward, painting each section in turn with vertical brushstrokes.

3. You will need to work quite quickly so that each section blends with the next.

YOU WILL NEED
- Dust sheet
- Paintbrushes
- Paint

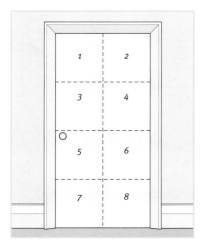

TRY IT

Keeping hinges clean

When painting a door, make sure not to paint over the hinges. If the screws are clogged with paint it will be difficult to remove them or make adjustments. Cover the hinges with tabs of masking tape to keep them paint free.

223 How to achieve a smooth finish

When painting a flush door, it is important that all the sections are blended together smoothly with each other. Any paint buildup between sections will dry to form a noticeable ridge.

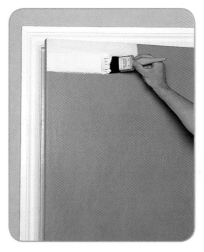

1. To ensure that the paint edge never dries out you must work quickly. Beginning in the top left-hand corner (or the right-hand corner if you are left-handed) apply the paint in horizontal strokes until the brush is empty. Reload the brush and continue horizontally until the section is complete.

2. To "lay off" the horizontal strokes in this first block, lightly load the brush with paint and, starting at the top, brush downward in vertical strokes until the section is complete. Now quickly move on to section two, situated alongside the first.

3. Start section three, picking up the bottom edge of block one. Use short vertical strokes to pick up the edge, then turn the brush around to make horizontal strokes to fill up the section. Lay off this block with vertical strokes as before. Continue painting each block until the door is complete.

4. Paint the opening edge of the door using a narrow brush. Start at the top and paint to the bottom of the door, taking care to blend the edges of the previously painted sections. It is only necessary to paint the top of the door if it can be seen from above.

Paint processes and systems: windows

Windows present a more difficult painting task than doors because they have so many different flat surfaces and moldings. In addition there are numerous glazed areas to consider; you can use strips of decorator's tape to mask off the edge or, if you have a steady hand, you can overlap the paint directly onto the glass.

224 Get ready for perfect painting

Painting windows takes time so leave plenty to get the job done properly. Try one window first and assess the timescale, and then make a work plan.

1. Mask off glass – Cut strips of decorator's tape and apply them to the edge of the glass, leaving a small gap between the tape and the frame. The gap will allow the paint to lap onto the glass, creating a seal that will protect the wood from any moisture or condensation that may collect on the glass surface.

2. Brush up your painting technique – Use a narrow paintbrush or a cutting-in brush with angled bristles to paint the glazing bars and frames. Always keep the wet edge next to the glass, and use a dabbing action to get paint into the corners of the moldings.

FIX IT

Tidying up paint edges

To clean up an untidy paint edge on a glass pane, use a metal ruler and a utility knife with a sharp blade. Cut along the straight edge, and peel away the ragged edge up to the cut.

225 Cleaning window furniture

It's a good idea to strip off all the paint from old window furniture if you intend to reuse it. Immerse small fittings in a small jar of chemical paint stripper or brush the stripper onto larger items such as window stays, then scrub away the loosened paint using a small wire brush.

FIX IT

Avoiding paint seals

After you have painted your sash windows, move the frames up and down several times during the drying period to keep them from sticking. Use the blade of a filling knife to do this to avoid touching the wet paint with your fingers and leaving finger marks.

TRY IT

Using a paint guard

A ragged and uneven paint finish on the window glass looks unsightly. Although using strips of masking tape to protect the glass is a good option, it can leave an edge that is prone to flaking and likely to be damaged by condensation. To avoid this, try using a handheld paint guard instead. These can be bought from home-decorating stores or you can simply make an improvised guard from a cereal box. Hold the blade of the guard a few millimeters away from the window frame and then apply the paint using a narrow brush. The paint will overlap the glass and form a weatherproof seal.

226 Painting sash and casement windows

In order to paint a window successfully you must first remove all the window furniture: handles, window stays and security hardware. Remember to keep all fixing screws safe.

YOU WILL NEED
- Paint
- Paintbrushes
- Masking tape

Casement windows

1. To begin, mask off the edges of the glazed section using decorator's tape (or use a painting guard); then paint the horizontal glazing bars on the fixed window of the casement. You will need to prop the hinged window sections open while you paint.

2. Next, paint the frames of the hinged opening sections. Remember that the outside edges should match the color of the exterior paint.

3. You can now paint the outer frame and the vertical center frame member that lies between the fixed casements. Finally, paint the windowsill and the rabbets in the frame that accommodate the hinged opening sections.

Sash windows

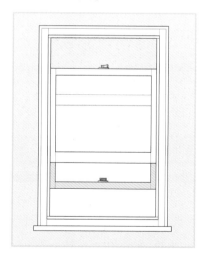

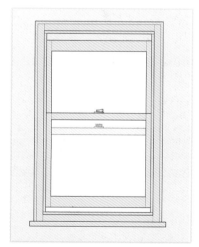

1. In order to paint a sash window without removing it from the frame you must begin by raising the inner (bottom) sash as far as it will go, and lowering the outer (top) one. Use a narrow brush to apply paint to the lower half and the bottom edge of the top sash. Now paint the exposed beads at the sides of the frame.

2. Let the paint become touch dry, then reverse the position of the sashes. Apply paint to the upper half of the top sash together with the topmost edge and the remainder of the exposed beads at each side.

3. You can now paint the outer frame and the vertical center frame member that lies between the fixed casements. Finally, paint the windowsill and the rabbets in the frame that accommodate the hinged opening sections.

Hanging new doors

You might want to replace a door because the old one is damaged or simply because you want one that is more attractive, more durable or in line with your new decor. New doors do not have hinges, locks or handles so you'll have to install those yourself.

227   How to make recesses for new hinges

If old paint is heavily layered, badly applied or chipped it should be completely stripped before repainting. Using a heat gun encourages the paint to blister and pull away from the wood so that you can easily scrape it away with a flat-bladed knife.

YOU WILL NEED
- Hinges
- Pencil
- Utility knife
- Chisel
- Mallet
- Electric drill
- Screws
- Screwdriver

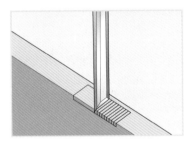

1. Prop the door up on its opening edge, and mark the position of the new hinges using a pencil. Score along the marked lines using a utility knife, then measure and score a line to match the depth of the hinge on the door face. Use the blade of the chisel to make a series of parallel cuts down to the line on the door face.

2. Use a chisel and mallet to chop out the shallow recess; then check the fit of the hinge and adjust if necessary. Place the hinge in the recess, and, using an electric drill, make pilot holes for the screws. Drive just one screw into the hinge to hold it in place. The remaining screws will be driven in later when the door is hung.

229   Foolproof door hanging

Prop the new door up on wedges with the hinges next to their positions on the door frame. Then slide the door closer to the frame so the hinges lie neatly in the recesses. It will be useful to have a helper to hold the door steady at this stage. Insert one screw into each hinge on the door frame. Check that the door swings smoothly and closes properly without binding, then insert the remaining hinge screws and tighten to secure.

228   Measuring up

- If you're replacing a door in an old house it could be a non-standard size. Try architectural salvage yards to find one that might be a close fit, then trim it down to size using a jigsaw or a plane.

- Remember that door frames are not always square; take measurements in two places for the width and three places for the height.

- Don't forget that doors vary in thickness; check that the new one is the correct thickness to fit the rabbet in the door frame.

- Always unwrap a new door and leave it in the room to acclimatize for a few days before hanging it.

TRY IT

Using a door wedge

When removing, hanging or repairing a door, hold it firmly in position with a wedge to keep it propped open. Open the door at a right angle to the frame, and then position a wedge at the side or end of the door, tapping it sharply with a hammer until it stops moving. Make sure you leave enough space to be able to pass through the door.

230 Fitting door handles

On interior doors all you will need is a simple spring latch operated by a handle on each side of the door. Fit the new handle to correspond with the old striker plate on the door frame, so you don't have to make a new recess.

YOU WILL NEED
- Handles
- Pencil
- Drill
- Spade bit
- Utility knife
- Chisel
- Mallet
- Screws

FIX IT

Trimming a latch spindle

If the spindle of the new latch is too long for a thin door, you may trim it to fit. Insert the spindle into the hole and fit the handles. Mark the amount to be cut off. Clamp the spindle to a workbench or sturdy work surface and cut it to the correct length using a hacksaw.

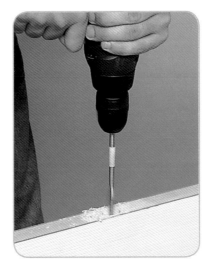

1. Mark the position of the handle on the door, and use a spade bit to drill a hole into the edge of the door to accommodate the latch body. Insert the latch and draw around the edge of the face plate with a pencil. Score, then chisel out a shallow recess to match the depth of the face plate.

2. Place the latch body on the door, with its face plate flush with the edge of the door. Mark the position of the spindle hole through the latch body, and do the same on the other side of the door. Drill a hole the same diameter as the spindle through the door.

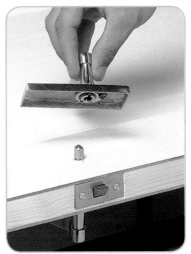

3. Fit the latch body into the edge of the door, and screw it into place. Insert the spindle and slip on the handle. Position the sides of the handle's face plate parallel with the door's edge. Drill pilot holes and screw the face plate to the door.

4. Turn the door over and slip the other handle over the exposed spindle. Position the face plate of the handle as in Step 3, drill pilot holes and screw the face plate securely to the door. You can now hang the door in the door frame.

Door furniture and security

Redecorating your home takes a lot of time and careful thought, and it's the finishing touches that can make all the difference. Old door furniture can spoil the look of a freshly painted door, so it's worth considering replacing handles and hinges as well as knobs and knockers. You may want to fit a front door with a door viewer or a door chain for added security.

231 Choosing new door handles

Door handles vary in size and style, but they usually fit any door. In general, door handles are sold in pairs and come with a spindle, which passes through the door and connects the handles, plus a set of fixing screws. If you choose vintage handles they may have lost their fixing screws; make sure that the new screws you choose match the finish.

- **Style** Door handles are both functional and decorative; they add character and complete your decorating theme. Choose a style that is in line with the total look of your home.

- **Finish** Look for easy-maintenance, easy-clean materials – chrome, brushed nickel and brass finishes are popular – but also consider your family lifestyle. Shiny chrome handles could perhaps be difficult to keep clean with lots of children in the house.

- **Budget** Count how many door handles you'll need before you make your choice. Good-quality hardware can be expensive, and the cost can quickly rise. It's useful to have a figure in mind when you go shopping.

- **Functionality** Do some of your rooms need a lock on the doors? Check that your chosen style has variations in functionality.

- **Ease of use** Consider how easy the handles are to use for the whole household, including children and the elderly. A door handle is no use at all if you can't operate it easily.

More compact, locking door handles can be used where space on the door frame is limited.

A door handle with an integral lock is useful when extra security is required. The wide variety of styles and finishes available make it possible to match existing door hardware.

TRY IT

Fitting knobs and knockers

Door furniture is both functional and decorative and can enhance the appearance of your front door. A sturdy door knob is useful to hold onto when closing the door, and rather than a doorbell, a knocker is a rather more traditional way of letting you know there's someone calling. Both are easily installed by drilling a hole through the door to accommodate the bolt fixing.

An ornate door knocker can look out of place on a simple modern door but can add a touch of class to a traditional or period-style home.

Brass door handles in high shine, matt and satin finish look stylish in traditional and more contemporary designs.

Chrome-finish door furniture works well for modern and minimalist designs.

Faux crystal handles combined with a chrome or brass finish creates a feminine, delicate style, suitable for a bedroom or elegant dining or living area.

232 Coat hooks

Coat hooks are handy for coats, bathrobes, laundry bags or towels – and anything else you may want to keep handy on the back of a door. It's an easy job to screw your hook into a solid door, but remember to use a self-drilling hollow door anchor to screw a hook to a hollow-core door.

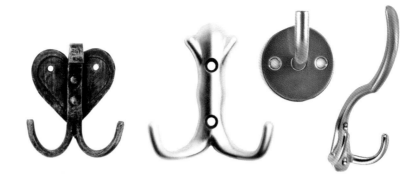

233 How to fit a door chain

This simple device allows the door to be opened partway in order to check a caller's identity before allowing them entry.

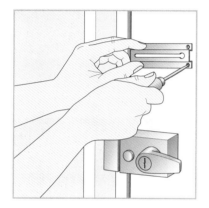

1. Screw in the plate track to the door next to the frame, and mark the screw hole positions using a bradawl. Make pilot holes using the bradawl, and then drive in the fixing screws securely.

2. Mark the position of the chain fixing on the door frame. It may be necessary to chisel away a shallow recess in the molding so the fixing plate lies flush with the door frame.

3. Mark and drive pilot holes into the frame using the bradawl, and then screw the chain fixing plate securely into place.

234 How to a fit a door viewer

This is also known as a fish-eye lens, and it allows you to see who's calling before you open the door.

Mark the position of the door viewer in the center of the door at eye level. Drill a hole from both sides of the door the same diameter as the outer sleeve of the viewer fitting. Unscrew the two sections of the viewer, and insert the lens from the outside and the viewing barrel from the inside. Screw both parts together.

FIX IT

Filling old screw holes

Unless you're very lucky indeed, the screw holes on the new fittings will probably not be in the same places as on the old ones. This is simple to remedy, by filling in the old holes with quick-drying filler. When the filler is dry, use abrasive paper to sand the filled areas smooth and flush with the surrounding door surface. The repaired holes will not show through when the new paint finish is applied. Remember to apply a spot of primer to the filled area, or it will show through as a dull patch on the new paint job.

DOOR AND WINDOW KNOW-HOW

TYPES OF INTERIOR DOOR

* **Panel doors** These are readily available as stock in home-decorating stores. Made from softwood or hardwood, they can be trimmed and planed to size quite easily. They usually have four, six or eight panels. They are relatively inexpensive and easily matched to existing features using paint or stain and varnish. Unusual designs may be expensive and hard to find.

* **Molded doors** Surface contours are made from wood, plastic or man-made fiberboard. They are inexpensive, but can look cheap. The advantage is an easy-clean, pre-finished, no-maintenance surface.

* **Flush doors** The timber framework is faced on both sides with a smooth man-made board. They can be trimmed and shaped to size but usually to a maximum of ¼ in (6 mm) at the sides and ⅜ in (10 mm) at the top and bottom. They are light, inexpensive and readily available. They have a contemporary feel and can look out of place in a period or traditional home but can be painted to match the decor, or may be finished with a veneer or molded panel.

* **Louver doors** Slats are fitted into the wooden frame to allow good ventilation.

* **Glazed panel doors** A wooden frame is set with single or multiple glazed panels. These can be useful in areas of low daylight.

TYPES OF WINDOW

Wood

* **Casement windows** These are wood-framed windows that usually have fixed panes combined with panes that are hinged on one edge to allow for opening.

* **Pivot windows** These contain a single "sash" or glazed frame. When opened, the top of the sash moves backward and the bottom forward, pivoting around the center.

* **Double-glazed windows** These have a wooden frame glazed with two panes with an air gap between.

* **Double-hung sash windows** These have traditional-style wooden-framed glazed "sashes" that slide up and down inside jambs at each side.

Metal and plastic

* **Steel windows** These can have poor insulating properties. Modern units arrive ready-finished and are low maintenance.

* **Aluminum windows** The slim profile of the frame can be manufactured in many different shapes. They are usually set into a wooden frame.

* **Plastic windows** These are uPVC windows and are usually white or brown. They are low maintenance but can degrade in sunlight.

How to choose new doors

Replacing interior doors is a decorating task well within the reach of the home decorator (see page 132). However, replacement windows are better left to a professional.

* Keep your budget in mind, but don't be tempted to compromise on quality.

* New doors are a long-term investment; think about co-ordinating your furniture and scheme to the doors rather than the other way around. Consider doors a permanent feature.

* Think, plan and measure carefully; once doors are cut and trimmed to size they can't usually be returned to the store. Mistakes can be costly.

* Doors are available in a multitude of styles. Choose a style to complement the other features of your home – sometimes traditional and contemporary works; sometimes it doesn't.

* Fully or partially glazed doors can be an option if your home lacks natural light.

* Consider the type of maintenance required. Do you want an easy-clean finish, or traditional wood that requires a little TLC from time to time?

* Is your choice restricted? Some building regulations require the use of fire doors, so you may have a limited choice of styles.

MATERIALS: WOOD, PLASTIC, METAL

238 The material you choose for a replacement window largely depends on your priorities. Choose wood if you prefer traditional-style natural materials and have a more flexible budget; vinyl if economy, energy efficiency and low maintenance are important; metal if you need something strong and durable.

- **Wood** An environmentally preferable option; it can be recycled and is biodegradable but can be very expensive.

- **Plastic (uPVC)** A man-made material that is less expensive than wood. These windows are energy efficient but are not recyclable and are hazardous to the environment if incinerated. While relatively maintenance free, old and faded uPVC units are unsightly and cannot easily be given a facelift.

- **Metal** Requires little maintenance, but due to good conductive qualities these windows tend to conduct heat away from the house, so they are less energy efficient. However they are durable, strong, resistant to temperature extremes and are not affected by sunlight. Metal is also suitable for very large windows.

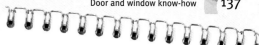

4 glass-cleaning tips

239 Windows always look so much better when they're clean.

- Dilute one part vinegar with four parts water, then use a sheet of crumpled-up newspaper to apply it to the glass. Buff in an S-shaped pattern to a streak-free shine.

- Beware of drips. Protect floors and carpets from detergent and water with a dust sheet or old towel when cleaning windowpanes or glazed doors.

- Steam cleaners make quick work of window cleaning. It may be worth the investment if you have lots of large windows. The small attachments are useful for windows with multiple small panes.

- Don't clean windows on a sunny day. The heat will dry the cleaning solution too quickly, leaving an unsightly streaky finish.

WEATHERPROOFING DOORS AND WINDOWS

240 If you're still feeling the cold when all the windows and doors are closed, then you should consider where the drafts are coming from. Weatherproofing is cheap and easy to install and can save on energy bills. It's worth it.

- An old-fashioned, sausage-shaped fabric draft excluder works well if your doors have gaps at the threshold. (If you've removed carpet in favor of wood floors, there may be a discrepancy, for instance.) You can co-ordinate with your color scheme, too.

- Threshold gaps can be sealed by using a fiber sweep. It looks like a long thin brush and can be nailed along the bottom of the door.

- Self-adhesive rubber weather stripping can be applied to the sides and top of the door casing to create a tight seal

when the door is closed. This can sometimes be applied with panel nails, and works for windows too.

- Sealant applied using a cartridge gun can be the answer for drafty windows. Examine the frames carefully to identify where the draft is coming from, then seal it up neatly.

- Curtains make a real difference to drafty doors and windows. Choose heavyweight fabric and insulated linings; you can swap to lighter-weight curtains in warmer seasons.

Window furniture and security

There are many reasons for replacing window furniture or hardware, but style and functionality are the two most common. You may choose to upgrade your hardware to a better or different finish or to one that complements a new decorating scheme. You may also decide to add security elements. Most window hardware can be installed quite easily using your basic toolbox.

FIX IT

Solving hinge problems

- A stiff or squeaky hinge can usually be fixed with a squirt of general-purpose household lubricating oil.
- Worn or rusty hinges must be replaced. Most are available in standard sizes, so you'll probably find that the new screw holes are in the same position as the old ones.

- Steel hinges must be primed and painted to keep them from rusting.
- Brass hinges won't rust and can be left unpainted; they look most attractive when used with other brass window hardware.
- Always use fixing screws that match the material of the hinge.

241   Types of window lock

Casement windows

- Lockable handle that replaces an existing casement handle.
- Locking stop to prevent the existing handle or casement stay from being operated without a key.
- Separate lock to hold the window shut.

Sash windows

- Dual screw inserted through the window frame that holds the two sashes together.
- Keyed and non-keyed sash locks, screwed onto the outside of the sash.

242   Securing window hardware

- If the screws securing window hardware are loose and will not retighten, replace them with slightly longer ones of the same diameter.
- If the recess of an old hinge bed is too deep for the new hinge, you can shim it with pieces of cardboard.

243   How to install a dual screw

This device is a threaded bolt that passes through both sashes where they meet at the center of the window, locking them together when engaged.

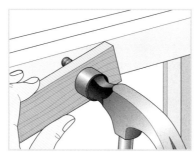

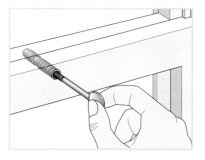

1. Mark a point halfway across the inner sash, then drill a hole to accommodate the screw barrel (the instructions will tell you the dimensions) through to the outer sash. The drill bit should penetrate the outer sash by about ¾ in (20 mm). Wrap a tab of masking tape around the drill bit as a depth gauge.

2. Tap the longer barrel of the device into the hole you just made in the inner sash, then reverse the sash positions in order to insert the shorter barrel into the outer sash. Use a scrap of timber between the hammer and the window frame to avoid damaging the paint surface.

3. Close the sashes and insert the locking bolt, plain end first, using the special key provided. The square end of the bolt should lie flush with the surface of the window frame.

244 How to install a sash lock

When closed, a sash lock of this type pulls the sashes together securely and keeps them from rattling in windy weather. These locks are available as keyed versions too.

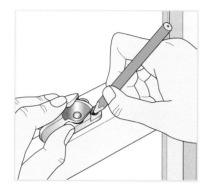

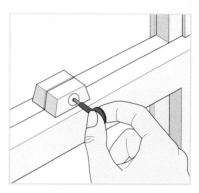

1. Position both halves of the new lock on the window where the sashes meet, resting each half on the appropriate sash. Use a pencil to mark the screw holes; then make a drilling guide hole using the point of a bradawl.

2. Make pilot holes for the screws using an electric drill. Screw each half of the sash lock securely into position. Try out the lock to make sure it operates correctly.

Surface locks are installed in the same way as sash locks but are operated with a key. When locked these devices cannot be tampered with from the outside.

FIX IT

How to fit new window hardware

Replacing stays and handles on a casement window is a quick and easy task. Simply remove the old ones and screw in the new ones. If the screw holes don't match, fill the old ones with a quick-setting filler, rub down with abrasive paper, then repaint or touch up the filled areas. Casement windows basically open and close like a door. They should be secured with locks or handles that fasten to the frame or with self-locking handles and stays.

• **Lockable casement handle** This lockable casement handle is fitted in the same way as an ordinary handle but has a keyed locking facility.

• **Lockable casement arm** A lockable casement arm is fitted so that the outer stay bracket lies on the bottom rail of the window. The casement arm should be in place so you can mark the bracket's position before screwing it in.

• **Casement lock** This two-part lock has a receiving bracket that is screwed to the frame and a bracket with an arm screwed to the window stile; to lock the window the arm swings over the receiving bracket.

Window treatments

Window treatments will probably be the last item on your home-decorating list of things to think about; however, whether you decide to make your own or buy ready-made curtains or blinds you will need to install the fixing brackets yourself.

246 Measuring up

- Measure your window space before choosing the track or pole to avoid disappointment if the fixing you like won't fit.

- Allow a minimum of 6 in (15 cm) on each side of the window recess to let in the maximum amount of daylight. If the curtains are very full, allow more. Narrow windows can be made to appear wider by extending the track on either side.

245 Removing fixings for decorating

You will need to remove all your old track or pole brackets when you're decorating. If you intend to reuse them, remember to keep all the screws and bits and pieces together in a plastic bag. Or, if you're installing new brackets, fill in all the old screw holes before painting or papering, as it is unlikely that the old holes will match the new fixing brackets.

FIX IT

Drilling into lintels

Windows have solid concrete lintels above them and these can be difficult to drill into. Here are three ways around this:
- Position the track/pole fixing brackets at least 9 in (23 cm) above the window recess, thus avoiding the lintel altogether. Make sure that your curtains will be long enough.

- Try fixing a timber batten to the wall using masonry nails, then screw the track or pole brackets to the batten. It will be easier than trying to screw directly into the lintel.

- If you have a low ceiling there may be no space above the lintel. You might consider mounting the track brackets onto the ceiling and securing the fixing screws into the joists.

TRY IT

Installing blinds

Blinds are purchased as a complete kit and can be installed inside or outside the window recess, usually using one bracket at each end.

- **Fixing the brackets inside a window recess** Brackets can be screwed directly to the window frame, the adjacent walls or to the underside of the top of the recess. Note: Do not screw brackets into uPVC window frames.

- **Fixing the brackets outside the window recess** See Drilling into lintels, left.

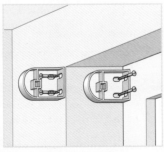 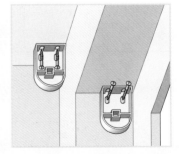

- **Fixing the brackets into masonry** Mark the screw hole position and drill clearance holes using a masonry bit. Insert screw anchors into the holes, and screw the brackets in place.

- **Fixing the bracket to the ceiling** You can screw the brackets directly to the joist if they are in the correct position.

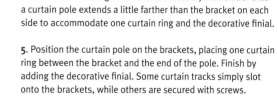

247 Installing a curtain pole or track in five easy steps

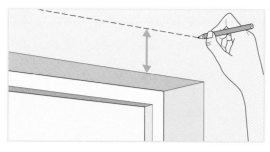

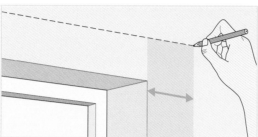

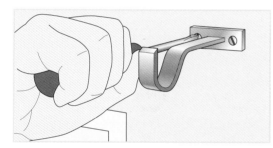

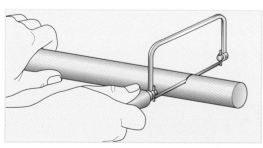

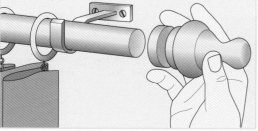

Curtain poles and tracks are usually purchased as a kit with the necessary fixings you'll need to install them. Choose one that is about 24 in (60 cm) longer than the window. All you'll need to do is measure the position carefully and drill a few holes to accept the fixing screws. Easy.

Note: Lightweight curtains can be hung from plastic tracks, but metal corded tracks are more suitable for heavier interlined curtains. Always ensure that the track is centered on the brackets.

YOU WILL NEED
- Tape measure
- Pencil
- Track or pole plus fixings
- Cable/pipe detector
- Drill
- Masonry bit
- Screw anchors
- Hacksaw
- Screwdriver

1. Decide how far above the window recess you'd like your track or pole to go, then measure and mark it using a faint pencil line. A measurement of 3–5 in (8–13 cm) is usually used, so that the heading tape cannot be seen from the outside.

2. The pole/track should extend at least 4–5 in (10–13 cm) from the window recess on both sides, in order to allow in as much light as possible when the curtains are drawn back. Mark the position of the end brackets.

3. Place the brackets in position and mark the screw holes using pencil dots. Test for cables and pipes, and then drill clearance holes using a masonry bit at the marked points. Insert screw anchors into the holes. Screw the bracket into position; a long pole may require an extra supporting bracket in the middle. Curtain track sometimes has several fixing brackets spaced evenly across the width of the window.

4. Raise the pole/track up to the brackets to check the length. Then cut to size using a hacksaw if necessary. Remember that a curtain pole extends a little farther than the bracket on each side to accommodate one curtain ring and the decorative finial.

5. Position the curtain pole on the brackets, placing one curtain ring between the bracket and the end of the pole. Finish by adding the decorative finial. Some curtain tracks simply slot onto the brackets, while others are secured with screws.

Finishing touches: crown molding

Finishing touches like crown molding, picture rails, chair rails and base boards will be the last things to consider in your decorating regime. If your home has these features already, then treat and prepare them as you would for wood (see page 60). If you don't, you might like to install some. Repair and installation is easy to do and these features may make all the difference to your new decor.

248 Types of crown molding

Crown molding is available in various materials and qualities; choose your product according to your budget. Always use the recommended adhesive for the type of crown molding you choose.

- **Fibrous plaster** The most expensive option. White, smooth, traditional and aesthetically pleasing. Heavy in weight and may require screw fixing in addition to adhesive. Will need priming before painting.

- **Polymer** Molded to look like plaster, but cheaper and lighter. Does not require priming before painting.

- **Wood** Useful where there are other wood features or partial wood wall claddings. Can be varnished or primed and painted.

- **Polystyrene** Very cheap, light and easy to fix, but can be fragile and easily damaged.

249 Cutting miters in crown molding

Crown molding is angled trim that bridges the joint between the walls and the ceiling. It can be fairly plain in design or quite ornate, and it can be made of wood, plaster or molded polymer. It is purchased in long straight lengths, so you will need to cut it to fit internal and external corners, using a miter saw or box. It is also easily damaged.

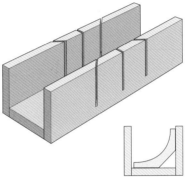 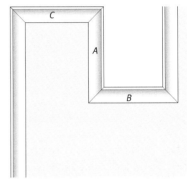

1. A miter box is made of three lengths of wood with diagonal slots cut across the two sides. Place the crown molding in the box and cut using the slots as your saw guide. Always place the ceiling edge of the crown molding on the base of the box.

2. Lengths of crown molding that have one internal and one external miter have parallel cuts made with the same slot (see A). Lengths with two external or internal corners (see B and C) are cut using both slots, one for each end.

3. The diagrams indicate the direction of the angled cut necessary for internal and external miters. Always remember to raise the crown molding to the wall and mark the direction of the cut first before cutting. Mistakes can be costly.

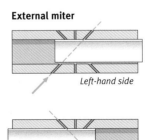 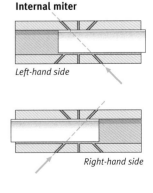

External miter

Left-hand side

Right-hand side

Internal miter

Left-hand side

Right-hand side

250 Installing new crown molding

Crown molding is an easy and decorative way of covering up an unsightly join between ceiling and wall. Usually the crown molding is painted the same color as the ceiling.

YOU WILL NEED

- Tape measure
- Pencil
- Shave hook
- Saw
- Miter box
- Adhesive spatula
- Panel nails
- Hammer
- Crown molding
- Construction adhesive
- Putty knife

1. Pencil in a guideline around the room on the walls and ceilings. Crosshatch the areas between the guidelines using the blade of a shave hook to provide a good key for the construction adhesive. For a plaster-type crown molding, you must remove any wallpaper within that marked area.

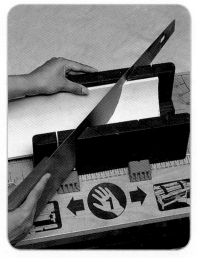

2. Start at the left-hand end of the longest wall in the room. Cut the correct miter (see Cutting miters in crown molding, opposite). The one shown here is for the right-hand side of an internal corner (or left-hand side of an external corner). Use the opposite angle for a left-hand internal corner (or right-hand external corner).

FIX IT

Repairing decorative crown molding

Minor damage to decorative plaster crown molding can be repaired using cellulose filler. Brush away loose sections and debris, then apply cellulose filler using a clay modeling knife. Use the tip of the knife to match the profile of the surrounding pattern, then let the filler dry.

3. Apply adhesive to the rear face of the crown molding and stick it into place. Use panel nails to support it temporarily while the adhesive sets. Miter and fit a matching length at the opposite end of this wall. Then fit lengths as required between the two end sections, carefully cutting the miters to size.

4. Start with the next wall, butting the mitered ends together and filling the joint with adhesive. For a chimney breast, cut miters on both ends and fit the crown molding for the back walls of the alcoves. Then fit the crown molding along the sides of the chimney breast, and, finally, the front.

Finishing touches: chair and picture rails

Picture rails and chair rails are made of wood and are similar in their appearance and method of installation; however, picture rails are situated anywhere from a few inches to a foot below the ceiling, while chair rails are placed approximately 3 ft (1 m) up a wall when measured from the floor. Picture and chair rails can provide a useful visual break for changes in paint color or wallpaper.

251   Fitting rails up a stairwell

If your rails are to follow a stairwell, measure and mark the height of the rail at right angles from the front of the stair tread at the top and bottom step. Now draw a straight line between the marks. Extend the line to join up with horizontal rails at the top and bottom of the slope then cut the miters to fit.

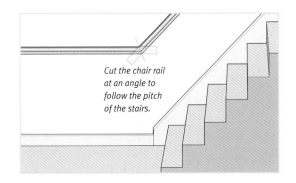

Cut the chair rail at an angle to follow the pitch of the stairs.

252   Securing rails

Never nail chair or picture rails into position; always use screws and screw anchors if necessary. If you're really in a hurry you can secure them in place using instant-grip adhesive. However, this is not advisable if you intend to hang pictures – use screw fixings instead.

FIX IT

Joining lengths

Straight cut lengths to fit between short walls with internal angles. You may need to butt join them to achieve the correct length for a long wall. Use wood adhesive to make the join secure. Fill any gaps with wood filler and sand smooth when dry.

FIX IT

Recessing screw heads

The diagram shows a secure screw fixing driven into a hole with a screw anchor. When drilling holes through rails, make sure that the recess will fall in an unobtrusive part of the profile molding as shown.

253 Foolproof installation of picture and chair rails

Picture rails are fixed to the walls above head height, and chair rails at around waist level. Picture rails allow pictures or mirrors to be hung without damage to the wall surface, and chair rails prevent scuffing from furniture, especially the backs of chairs.

YOU WILL NEED

- Spirit level
- Pencil
- Tape measure
- Power drill and suitable bit
- Countersink bit plus masonry bits
- Screwdriver
- Countersunk screws
- Screw anchors if required
- Coping saw
- Tenon saw
- Miter box
- Panel nails
- PVA adhesive
- Putty knife
- Filling compound

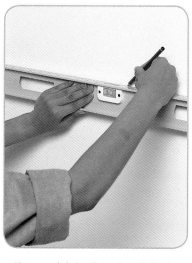

1. Picture and chair rails are installed in the same way, using screws and screw anchors or just screws for drywall. Start by drawing a horizontal pencil guideline around the room at the level required. Use a spirit level to ensure a true horizontal plane.

2. Drill clearance and countersink holes through the rail at 24 in (60 cm) intervals. Hold a length to the wall in the correct position with one end in an internal corner, and mark the screw hole positions. Drill the holes in the wall and insert a screw anchor if necessary. Screw the length to the wall with the screw heads recessed in the rail.

FIX IT

Using knotting solution

Knots in wooden moldings can be a decorator's nightmare, and can really spoil the appearance of a nice long stretch of painted trim. Use knotting solution to block stains and wood filler to repair small holes or cracks. However, if the knot is black, it is old and dry and may be loose. Pry out a loose knot and repair the hole with wood filler.

3. Butt join the rails until they reach the next internal corner. Trace the rail profile onto the end of the next length; cut it to shape with a coping saw. Repeat the stages in Step 2 to fix the rails to the wall, then continue around the room.

4. At external corners, cut miters at a 45-degree angle on the rails, using a tenon saw and miter box. Glue and nail the joins once they have been fixed to the wall; this keeps them from opening up in future. Finally, fill screw holes with wood filler.

TRY IT

Great gadget

A laser level is the perfect gadget for marking long, straight, perfectly horizontal lines.

Finishing touches: base boards

Your last port of call working down your walls from the crown molding will be the base boards. Base boards are a decorative yet functional molded trim added to the base of a wall; they can be plain or elaborate and are secured to the wall using nails, screws or adhesive. Here are a few tips to show you how to repair and replace base boards.

254   Types of base board

- These are usually made from softwood, with one square edge and one rounded or elaborately shaped and molded edge to reflect period-style decor.

- You can buy MDF moldings too. The advantage of these is that they are usually sold primed and ready for painting, and they don't have imperfections such as the knots or grain associated with wood trim.

TRY IT

Installing a door stop

Fix a door stop to base boards behind doors to prevent accidental scuffing and damage to the board from the door frame. In addition a door stop will prevent damage from the door knob on the wall above.

TRY IT

Scribing and mitering

Before installing new base boards, make a sketch of the room to help you plan how the ends will have to be cut and the order of installation.

1. Use an offcut of base board to trace the profile on the end of a straight-cut piece. Use a coping saw to cut along the traced line. Butt the first straight piece into an internal corner, then fix the second scribed piece over it.
2. Install base boards in the order shown here to ensure that any joints made using the scribing method will not be too obvious. Miter external corners and scribe internal corners.

External mitered corners

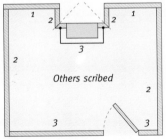

Others scribed

255   Tailored miters

Your walls may not be truly square, so external miters may require a bit of shaping to size using abrasive paper and a sanding block.

Cracks and imperfections

- **Spotting imperfections** It's easy to miss surface imperfections on long, flat, painted stretches of woodwork such as base boards. Simply shine a flashlight at a shallow angle across the surface; and you will easily spot lumps and bumps and any other little blemishes. Circle them with a pencil so you don't miss them.

- **Applying sealant** For a crack above a base board or around a window or door, squeeze a bead of sealant along it, making sure that the sealant contacts both surfaces. A slow continuous movement will avoid creating ripples in the bead; use a wet fingertip to smooth out the sealant when the gap is filled.

- **Filling a hole or dent** Mix up a small amount of wood filler and push it onto the surface using a flexible filling knife. Press down onto the damaged area then pull the knife toward you and away from the board. After the filler is dry, sand it level with the surrounding surface.

256 Removing base boards

You may want to replace your old boards, or simply move them to accommodate new flooring. To begin, run the blade of a utility knife along the join between the wall and the base board to break the seam of paper or paint. If you plan to refit the boards, pry out all of the nails and fixings first.

YOU WILL NEED
- Cold chisel
- Mallet
- Wooden wedges
- Crowbar
- Scraps of wood

1. Large nails will have been used to fix the board to masonry. Use a chisel and a mallet to pry the board away from the wall. Starting at an external corner or door, place the chisel behind the board, and hit it with the mallet. Use a wedge to hold it away from the wall.

2. Insert a crowbar into the gap, then slip a scrap of wood behind it to protect the wall. Gently press the crowbar back to move the board away from the wall for about 3 ft (1 m). Repeat the process, moving along the board until it comes away from the wall completely.

257 Perfectly installed base boards

Base boards protect the walls from furniture scuffs and damage from vacuum cleaners, and generally provide a decorative footnote to your walls. Boards can be fixed using nails or screws with screw anchors.

YOU WILL NEED
- Replacement base board
- Tenon saw • Wood glue • Hammer
- 2 in (50 mm) long oval nails
- Stud detector (optional)
- Nail punch • Filler • Filling knife

1. You will require a join for long walls. Make a scarf joint by cutting each end of the board with a tenon saw at a 45-degree angle. Apply a little wood glue to the joint, and fix to the wall at a stud point or to a wood block in a masonry wall.

2. Nail the boards to the walls using long oval nails. On drywall, drive the nails into the studs. Use a stud detector (if you have one) to locate them. For masonry walls, mark the location of the wood blocks. They will be set into the walls on the boards after they are cut. You can nail directly into the blocks.

3. Use a nail punch to drive each nail below the surface of the base boards. Once all the boards are in place, use wood filler to disguise the holes and to fill any joints and gaps in miters.

Shelving

You can never have too much storage space, and shelving is an ideal way to make use of wall space. There are several different methods of creating shelving, and all are easy if you know how. Here are a few tips and handy hints for installing shelves and making secure wall fixings.

TRY IT

Installing shelf brackets

If you just need a single shelf on an open wall then shelf brackets will do the job, and they come in a variety of functional and decorative styles. Decide where you want your shelf, then use a spirit level and a pencil to mark the position. Space the brackets evenly, one at each end and one in the center if the shelf is long. Then secure the first bracket to the wall.

1. Raise the shelf bracket to the wall and mark the screw hole positions. Drill holes in the wall and insert screw anchors if necessary. Secure the bracket in position, making sure it is perfectly horizontal.

2. Rest the edge of the shelf on the first bracket, then place the level on top to check the horizontal. Mark the position of the second bracket, and then secure as before. Lay the shelf on both brackets, and screw securely from the underside.

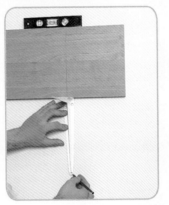

258 Shelving categories

- **Fixed-bracket** Shelf brackets are secured to the wall, and the shelf is then laid horizontally across the brackets.

- **Adjustable** Adjustable shelving systems can be very useful. Vertical rails are secured to the walls, and the shelf brackets can then be positioned at different heights – and repositioned.

- **Built-in alcove shelves** These are a popular choice for the home decorator. Support battens are secured across the back and sides of the alcove and the shelf laid on the battens.

259 Make the fixings strong enough

Fully loaded shelves exert a considerable force on the wall fixings. On solid masonry or plaster, use screws at least $1\frac{1}{2}$ in (38 mm) long, and drive them into screw anchors inserted into drilled holes. On timber-framed walls, locate the stud and then drive a screw securely through the drywall and into the timber. You can use cavity wall fixings such as spring toggles to mount shelves to drywall, but do this only if the shelf is intended to bear a light load.

260 Notching the shelf

When using adjustable shelving you may need to create a notch in the shelf to accommodate the track so that the back edge sits flush with the wall. Mark the position of the notch with a pencil, and then use a tenon saw to cut down the sides. Clamp the shelf securely to a workbench using a scrap of wood underneath. Hold the blade of a chisel perpendicular to the shelf, and tap the handle with a hammer or mallet to cut between the first two cuts. Remove the waste little by little, and sand the cut edges smooth.

TRY IT

Installing tracks and brackets

You could use a simple shelving system that comprises two (or more) wall-mounted vertical tracks into which the shelf brackets are slotted. Shelves do not need to be trimmed to size, as the ends are usually open.

1. Secure the tracks to the wall, making sure that they align with each other both vertically and horizontally. Slot each shelf bracket into position at the correct height.

2. When all the brackets are in position, lay each shelf in place. Use a spirit level to ensure the ends align with each other.

3. It is best to secure the shelves to the brackets. Lay the shelf across the brackets, and drive the screws upward from the underside (support the top of the shelf with your free hand). Make sure the screws are the correct length to penetrate the shelf to about two-thirds of its thickness.

261 Three steps to good drilling technique

In order to make sound wall fixings you will need to drill holes. Always use masonry bits for solid walls, and follow these simple steps.

1. For plaster-coated walls, drill slowly on low speed until you reach the solid wall under the plaster. You can now switch the drill to the hammer function in order to penetrate the masonry.

2. Mark and measure the position of each hole carefully. Use a spirit level as a guide if more than one hole is required. Use a large nail and a hammer to "spot" the hole positions. This creates a small hole so the drill bit will not slip out of position.

3. You do not need to drill a hole deeper than necessary. In order to drill to the correct depth, fit a rubber depth guide to the drill bit or simply wrap a tab of masking tap at the level required. Make sure the drill is at right angles to the wall before engaging the motor.

FIX IT

Putting up a short shelf

A short shelf that only requires two brackets is easier to install by first securing the brackets to the shelf with screws. You can use a straight edge or a batten to help align the back of the shelf with the back of the brackets. With the bracket in place, hold the shelf the right way up against the wall, and align it horizontally with a spirit level to mark the positions for the screws. Drill the holes for the screws and secure the brackets to the wall.

262 How to countersink fixings

Shelf battens are secured with screw fixings at several points along the length. However, the screw heads can look unsightly. Countersinking involves creating a recess that the screw head lies in, hiding it below the surface of the batten.

YOU WILL NEED
- Twist drill bit to match the screws
- Countersink bit
- Wood filler
- Filling knife
- Sandpaper

1. Drill a pilot hole through the batten using a straight twist bit. Make sure to match the diameter of the bit to the size of your screw. You can use the drill hole as a guide for the pointed tip of the countersink bit.

2. Remove the twist bit, and replace it with the countersink bit in order to enlarge the drill hole. As the countersink bit is driven into the wood, the widening diameter cuts a cone-shaped recess on the surface.

3. Insert a screw with a countersunk head into the drilled hole and drive it in using a screwdriver. Tighten the screw so the batten is secure and the head lies just below the surface of the surrounding wood.

NOTE: In order to make the screw fixings unobtrusive and really neat, fill the countersunk recess with wood filler and allow to dry. Sand the filler areas smooth, then apply primer and a paint finish of your choice.

263 Fixing shelves to a solid wall

- Solid walls are usually made of brick, concrete or block. Choose suitable fixings according to wall structure and item weight.

- Choose a screw that is the depth of the plaster plus the item thickness plus approximately 1¼ in (36 mm).

- Always use a masonry bit.

- Use a tab of tape around the drill bit to indicate the desired drill depth. You will need to drill deep enough so the screw anchor sits flush with the wall.

- Position the item, and drive in the screws to secure it to the wall. Do not overtighten the screw.

264 Fixing shelves to a hollow wall

- A hollow wall has a timber framework, which is covered with a drywall sheet. Secure fixing should be made, ideally, by screwing directly into the timber frame.

- Use a stud detector to locate the timber studs.

- If a stud is not in the right place for your fixture, use a spring toggle, drywall screw anchor, self-drilling drywall anchor or other suitable anchor fixings.

- Always match the item weight with the load of the wall fixing.

- The manufacturer will advise on the correct size hole to make to accept the fixing: too small and it won't fit; too large and it will fall out.

 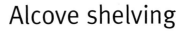

Alcove shelving

Alcoves provide the ideal opportunity to install a few shelves – you'll need to secure timber battens to the walls as support and then cut the shelf to fit. The shelf simply slots into place, resting neatly on the battens.

265 How to prepare battens

Timber battens are fixed to the side walls to support each end of the shelf, and in order to increase the shelf's load-bearing capacity, an extra batten can be fixed along the back wall. Use battens that are 1½ in x ⅜ in (38 mm x 10 mm), and secure them to the wall using 2 in (50 mm) screws with matching screw anchors. Generally, alcoves have solid walls because they tend to be positioned on either side of a chimney breast, but be sure to use cavity wall fixings if your alcoves are not solid.

YOU WILL NEED

- Tape measure
- Batten
- Tenon saw
- Sandpaper
- Paintbrush
- Primer
- Paint
- Pencil
- Drill with suitable bits
- Countersink bit

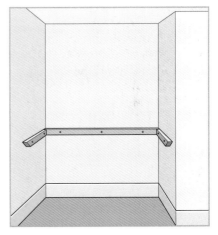

1. Measure the back wall and cut a batten to fit snugly between the side walls. Now measure and cut the side battens, taking the depth of the back batten plus 2 in (50 mm) from the measurement. The leading edge will sit short of the front edge of the shelf and therefore will not be too noticeable.

2. Use a saw to miter the leading edge of each side batten; this also helps hide the end. Use sandpaper to smooth off all the cut edges. Prime all the bare timber, and then paint to match the wall color.

3. Mark and drill three clearance holes across the length of the back batten, and two through each side batten. Countersink each screw hole so the fixing screws will lie flush with the surrounding timber (see opposite page). If you need to secure the shelf to the batten, mark and drill these holes too, making sure that they do not interfere with the fixing screws.

TRY IT

Installing floating shelves

"Floating" shelves are a particularly attractive design feature. They appear to float because the brackets are hidden inside the shelf. Most are purchased as a kit and will include all the necessary fixings. Simply secure the bracket in the form of a metal plate with protruding posts; the shelf has a receiving plate built in that sits snugly on the posts.

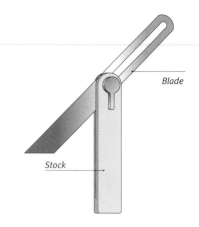

266   How to cut a shelf that fits

If you're installing shelves into alcoves, chances are the side walls won't be exactly at right angles to the back, and they won't be the same as each other, either! Use a sliding bevel to calculate the correct angles you'll need to cut the shelf to size.

YOU WILL NEED
- Tape measure
- Shelf
- Pencil
- Ruler
- Sliding bevel
- Jigsaw
- Sandpaper
- Paintbrush
- Primer and paint or stain and varnish

Blade

Stock

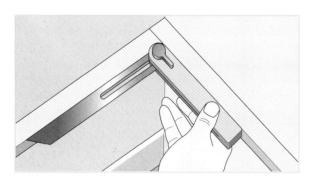

Use a sliding bevel to measure internal angles accurately.

1. After you have installed the support battens, measure the width across the back wall, and then measure between the walls at the front of the alcove. You will probably notice a slight difference. You will need to cut each side at a slightly different angle to ensure a snug fit.

2. Buy or cut a shelf a little wider than the widest measurement and to the depth required. Indicate the midpoint, then mark the correct width across the back edge. Place the handle of the sliding bevel on the back batten; then open up the blade so it lies along the side wall. This will form the angle you'll require to make the first cut.

3. Now place the bevel on one side of the shelf at one of the marked points along the back edge, using the bevel blade as a guide and the pencil and ruler to draw the correct side angle. Do likewise on the other side. Cut the angled side edges carefully using a jigsaw.

4. Try the shelf for size in the alcove, and, if necessary, make a few adjustments so it sits snugly on the battens. Use sandpaper to smooth off any rough edges along the jigsaw cut. Prime, paint or stain according to your decorating choice.

FIX IT

Hiding shelf battens

Fixing a batten along the front edge of the shelf obscures the end of the supporting battens attached to the side walls. Cut the batten to fit under the leading edge of each shelf. Clamp it in place using scraps of wood to protect the surfaces. Drive screws long enough to penetrate up through the batten but only two-thirds of the way through the shelf. Apply wood filler to the join between batten and shelf to disguise the crack.

267   "Floating" alcove shelves

If you have installed shelves at intervals all the way up your alcove, you can sometimes see the unsightly support battens from underneath. To avoid this, secure a batten along the front edge on the shelf, then use panel nails to fix a sheet of hardboard cut to size underneath. This results in a "floating" effect and creates a neat finish. Fill any gaps with wood filler then paint the top and underside to co-ordinate with your room decor.

268 How to put up shelves in an alcove

Alcoves are ideal for built-in shelving because the side walls can provide the support required. A batten can also be secured along the back wall to support heavier loads. Mark the position of each shelf with a pencil line.

YOU WILL NEED

- Softwood battens
- Tenon saw
- Tape measure
- Pencil
- Drill and bits
- Screw anchors

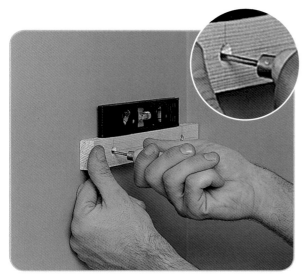

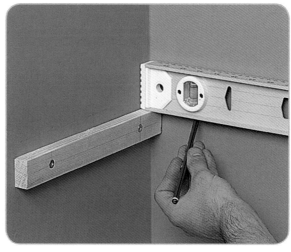

1. Cut the battens to fit the side walls, and then miter the leading end. Drill two holes through each one about 1 in (25 mm) from each end, position it on the wall, check it is horizontal and mark the screw holes. Drill the holes and insert screw anchors if necessary. Screw the batten securely to the wall.

2. Secure all the battens to the first wall. Balance a spirit level on each one in turn to mark a horizontal line across the alcove to the facing wall. Secure corresponding battens to the second wall and across the back wall if necessary.

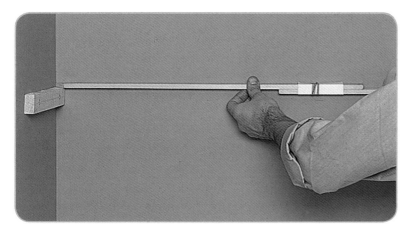

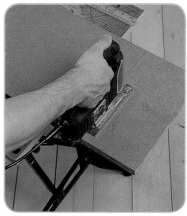

3. Measure each shelf separately using guide rods – two pieces of batten held together with rubber bands – to find the width of the back wall (this is more reliable than a retractable tape). Use a sliding bevel to find the correct angle of each corner.

4. Transfer the measurements to each shelf and cut them to size. You can paint each shelf at this stage. Let them dry before setting the shelves on the battens. Try not to scuff the paint on the side walls when you drop the shelves in place.

5 Essential maintenance and services

Regular maintenance is up there at the top of the home decorator's "to do" list alongside planning and preparation! Paint, paper, tiles, hardware and all the other beautiful surface treatments you have carried out and adornments you have installed will not stay looking fresh and new for ever without a little bit of care and attention. It's not difficult — you just need to remember to do it. It is far better to plan for emergencies and anticipate problems than be unprepared and taken by surprise.

Hardware maintenance

Replacing door and window furniture and other hardware is an important part of the home decorating process, however, these fixtures and fittings do not look after themselves. You need to spend a little time each year making sure that everything is clean, shiny and well lubricated! Prevention is better than cure.

269 Lubricants

Apply lubricants sparingly. Too much oil can attract dirt and dust, giving rise to more problems in the future. Wipe away any excess with a clean cloth.

272 Taking care of hinges

Doors and windows take a lot of rough treatment, so aim to give them a little attention once a year in order to keep them squeak free and working smoothly. Arm yourself with a can of penetrating spray lubricant, a paintbrush, an old rag and your toolbox. Interior doors typically have two or three hinges. Inspect each hinge and brush away any dirt or dust before spraying the central pin area with oil. Open and close the door/window until a smooth action is resumed or the squeak disappears. Wipe away excess oil using a dry rag.

270 Window hardware maintenance

• Open the window and vacuum out any dust or debris that may have built up in the rabbets over the years.

• Locks and hinges that are stopped with paint are no use at all. Unscrew the hardware, and soak them in paint stripper to remove the offending paint layer. Wash clean, lubricate and reinstall.

• Casement windows have stays, crank handles and hinges, and all are likely at some point to grind to a halt or get noisy or stiff. Open and close the window to locate the problem; then clean and lubricate.

• Metal or vinyl windows rarely require lubrication, but if you notice a problem, simply apply a light coating of silicone spray to the working parts or sash channels.

• Wooden sash windows can bind a little in the frame. A traditional fix is to rub a block of paraffin wax along the groove where the sash runs.

271 Door handle maintenance

• Stainless steel is a relatively low-maintenance material, but a door handle comes into contact with all sorts of grease, grime, sweat and general wear and tear that can cause the finish to dull. Use a soft cloth and a warm solution of detergent and water to revive it. Try adding a little vinegar for extra shine.

• Chrome is a popular choice for homeowners who prefer a modern, contemporary style; chrome can be matte, brushed or highly polished. Clean with a soft cloth and polish with wax occasionally to maintain.

FIX IT

Securing retaining screws

An annual inspection of the retaining screws that secure door hinges, handles, window stays and other door or window furniture will ensure that when you need them to work – they do. Wobbly door handles do eventually come off, and windows bind in the frame. Repair loose screw holes with wood filler (see page 66), and spray all moving parts with a little light oil from time to time.

273 Top brass-cleaning tips

Lots of door and window hardware is made of brass, and while it's lovely when its new and shiny, it tends to discolor over time. Avoid harsh abrasives. Instead, try these remedies to brighten dull brass.

- **Ketchup** Wipe ketchup onto the brass surface. When dry, remove using an old toothbrush. Buff to a shine with a soft cloth.

- **Worcestershire sauce** Use a damp cloth to apply the sauce; then buff the metal to a shine.

- **Lemon and baking soda** Cut a lemon in half and sprinkle baking soda onto it. Use this to rub the brass. Rinse off with warm water and buff.

- **Olive oil** Simply apply with a soft cloth and polish to a shine.

- **Onions** Chop an onion and simmer in water for two hours. Now use the remaining liquid to polish the brass hardware.

- **Plain yogurt** Cover the brass with yogurt and let dry. Rinse, then dry and buff with a soft cloth.

- **Toothpaste** Mix some toothpaste with a little water, and use it to polish the brass with a soft cloth.

FIX IT

Remedy for loose screws

During a routine check, make sure hinge screws on doors and casement windows are snug and secure. If when tightening a screw you find that it simply rotates without tightening, the screw hole may have become too large for the screw due to wear. Unscrew the hinge, then use wood glue to stick a short section of a wooden toothpick into the hole. Reinsert the screw when the glue is dry; the toothpick will give the screw thread a little extra grip so it can be tightened up again.

274 Taking care of door locks

Seasonal climate changes herald the kind of problems that are annoying, but easy to avoid: stubborn locks that stick and require a significant degree of "heft" to operate are typical. Promise yourself that once a year you'll do a maintenance check. Brush away dirt from the keyhole, then spray with oil. Now spray the key. Try opening and closing the lock a few times. This should fix the problem, but if not, carefully disassemble the lock and lubricate it more thoroughly before reassembly.

Maintenance and safety

An annual walk-around maintenance check is a way to keep on top of decorative and functional repairs as well as odd jobs in the home. It is better to fix things sooner rather than later, as a small job can often escalate into a bigger, more costly procedure. Check for drafts, leaks, peeling paint, air bubbles, lifting seams in the wallpaper, mold and dampness; check that radiators are working correctly; test the efficiency of battery-operated safety devices. Take a notebook with you to jot down anything you need to remember to do or add to the shopping list.

275 How to install a smoke/carbon monoxide detector

Carbon monoxide detector

Smoke detector

It is an easy task to install a smoke/carbon monoxide detector, and it could save lives. Lots of households choose battery-powered alarms, and these are the ones described here; mains-powered alarms are available, though they have to be fitted by a qualified electrician. It's a good idea to let everyone in the family know where the detector is, what the alarm sounds like and to formulate an escape routine in case of an emergency.

Location

- It is recommended that smoke detectors are mounted high on a wall or on a ceiling away from drafts from windows or doors. Smoke rises, so the detector should sound an alert at the first possible instance. Allow a gap of approximately 4 in (10 cm) between the unit and the corner of the wall or ceiling. Install smoke detectors on every level of your home, in hallways and near bedrooms. Avoid putting them in kitchens or laundry areas because the regular heat and steam will set detectors off frequently.

- Carbon monoxide dissipates evenly through the atmosphere in a room. Choose an alarm location that is easily accessible but out of reach of children, where the unit will stay clean and dry. Place them near heating systems and gas furnaces.

Installation

- Follow instructions and use the fixings provided. Measure the distance between the fixing holes on the mounting plate.

- Choose and indicate your location with pencil marks where the fixing holes should be.

- Drill holes to accept the fixing screws at the marked position. Remember to use a cable/pipe detector if you suspect hidden cables or pipework.

- Secure the mounting plate in position, and then assemble the unit as per the manufacturer's instructions.

Maintenance

- Push the test button regularly, in order to activate the alarm to ensure the batteries are still functional. Replace if the alarm does not sound or if it is too faint to be of use.

- Change batteries twice a year, in spring and fall, for example.

- Carbon monoxide detectors use chemical indicators, which will also need to be replaced. Check the indicator whenever you check the battery.

FIX IT

How to bleed a radiator

Every now and then you will need to bleed a radiator; this releases air pockets and ensures an even heat. An indication that an air pocket may be present is if the radiator is cold at the top and warm at the bottom.

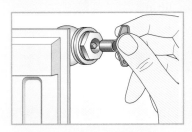 

1. You'll need a square-ended bleed key, readily available from a hardware store. Engage the key in the valve and turn in a counterclockwise direction.

2. You will hear the hiss of air escaping. Have a cloth or container at the ready to catch any water that may escape when the air has been expelled. Now close the valve.

276 How to check windows and doors

- Weather stripping is a cheap and efficient way to prevent drafts and to ultimately decrease your energy bills. It does not last forever, but it is easy to replace.

- Paint, varnish or stain finishes can deteriorate; check the condition of the window/door surfaces for signs of bubbling, peeling, flaking or cracks. Refinish if necessary.

- Check all moving parts such as locks, handles, stays and hinges; lubricate or replace.

- Windows or doors that are inoperable or beyond repair should be replaced.

277 Other things to watch out for

- **Leaking radiators** These can damage flooring, and moisture can seep through to ceilings below. Check that yours are sound.
- **Soft window and door frames** Test frames with your fingernail. If they are solid then there's no problem; if the surface of the wood is soft you may have a rot problem.
- **Ceiling stains** Dark stains on ceilings may indicate a leak. Locate the problem first, and then mask the stain before redecorating. The source may be a water pipe or simply unsound grout or sealant in the bathroom.
- **Holey woodwork** If you see small dark holes in your woodwork, you have woodworm – treat it immediately. It can attack furniture and floorboards.
- **Condensation, damp and mold** Ventilate your home regularly to guard against these plus lingering smells.

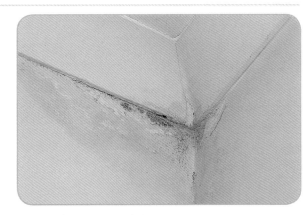

Mold caused by poor ventilation.

Holes characteristic of woodworm.

Odd jobs and fixes

If you have dampness or condensation problems, it's a good idea to identify the cause and remedy it before you carry out any redecoration projects. However, if you have moved into a new home during the summer months and completed redecorations when the weather was fine these problems may not be evident until the season changes and the cold, damp weather returns. Damp, condensation and mold will ruin newly decorated surfaces, so you'll need to repair them fast.

278   What is condensation?

Condensation is formed when warm, moist air hits a cold surface; the water vapor in the air turns into water droplets, which coat the surface. It is most common on windows, but can occur on walls and tiled areas too. The moist layer encourages black mold growth, which is unsightly, unhealthy and damaging to your interior decor.

- **Bathrooms and kitchens** These are two rooms where steam and moisture are most likely to cause a problem. Try to let steam escape through a window, or install extractor fans.
- **Bedrooms** Mold sometimes forms behind furniture (such as large wardrobes) that is situated next to cold external walls. Try to move the furniture to another wall, or leave a larger gap between the item and the wall to allow good ventilation.
- **Windows** This is a tricky problem to fix because glass is a poor insulator and can get cold at night. Generally the interior is warm, so condensation forms and mold tends to grow in the join between pane and frame. If double glazing is not an option, consider repainting the frames and allowing the paint to overlap the glass by a few millimeters. This creates a smooth seal and is less likely to collect moisture, which will discourage mold growth. It's easier to clean, too.

279   How to prevent condensation

Prevention is key so try these few proactive tips to stop condensation before it starts.

- Check that all caulking, sealants and glazing putty are sound and unbroken. Cracks and gaps allow in drafts, cold air and moisture. Perform regular maintenance checks, and make repairs as soon as you spot a problem.
- Always draw back your drapes and open the window blinds during hours of daylight. This allows air to circulate freely and encourages condensation to evaporate from the window surface, preventing a buildup of moisture and black mold growth.
- Recognize high-moisture problem areas, such as kitchens, bathrooms and laundry rooms. Ensure adequate ventilation exists, and check that all air vents are free and clear from debris and blockages.
- Cracks in exterior walls and floors in basements or cooler utility rooms may contribute to higher humidity levels in your home. Make repairs fast and monitor the differences in condensation levels.

280   How to tell if it's damp or condensation

The symptoms of condensation are random damp patches on walls, which become worse in cold weather, and black mold. To distinguish between damp and condensation, dry the damp area with a hairdryer, then place a piece of aluminum foil over it, sealed to the wall on all sides with duct tape. Moisture should form on the foil after a few days. If it is on the room side then the problem is condensation; if it is on the wall side then it is penetrating damp (see page 44).

TRY IT

Why use a dehumidifier?

Dehumidifiers draw moist air from the room, which then condenses on a set of coils inside the unit. The water then collects in a reservoir. Dry, cool air can then be passed over a set of heated coils and returned to the room by a fan. These units are useful for regular use in damp environments to stabilize the atmosphere.

281   Causes of condensation

Condensation is unpleasant and can lead to more significant problems. Learn to identify causes by recognizing the symptoms, and then carry out the appropriate fix.

SYMPTOMS	CAUSE	FIX
• Widespread condensation	Inadequate heating	Provide more heating.
• Condensation in room where the heater is used	Oil heaters	Abandon oil heater in favor of another form of heating.
• Damp and widespread mold growth on walls and ceilings	Lack of insulation in ceiling or wall cavities	Install insulation.
• Water dripping from the pipe and collecting under the pipe's pathway • Water can collect in pools	Unlagged pipes	Use foam lagging tubes on all cold-water pipes.
• Fogged windows • Mold growth around the edge of the frame	Glazing	Install double glazing if the problem is severe. Repaint frames, or apply secondary glazing.
• Damp stains appearing on walls of the chimney breast	Unused/sealed fireplaces	Ensure adequate ventilation through the flue via air bricks. Apply damp-blocking product to the stain before redecorating.
• Debris, insulation, furniture and so on may block ventilation bricks and other airways	Blocked airways	Clear all airways.
• Widespread condensation due to moisture release from fresh plaster, paint or wallpaper application	Building work	Allow plenty of time and ventilation for the works to dry out naturally.

282   How to deal with mold

Mold can grow quite rapidly in damp atmospheres such as kitchens or bathrooms and in little-used, poorly ventilated rooms. It's unsightly and can ruin your new decor. It usually presents as black or gray spots in isolated patches, but sometimes it can cover large areas. Here's what you can do to prevent mold attacks in your home.

• Mold is a fungus that loves dark, damp environments. Allow plenty of light into your home, and make sure there's adequate ventilation to release damp air.

• Using commercial cleaners to remove mold from painted surfaces can be an instant fix, but do try a test area first in case it removes the finish too.

• Ceiling fans are a good way to keep the air circulating.

• Dehumidifiers can be useful in dark basement areas where dampness is likely to be a problem.

• Due to their poor insulation properties, aluminum windows can be prone to mold growth. During cold weather, warm air inside your home readily forms condensation on the cold window frame and glass. Clean the frames and panes with a mixture of 1 tablespoon of household bleach and a gallon of water to inhibit mold growth.

• Cleaning metal window frames with rubbing alcohol can also discourage mold growth.

Odd jobs: tiling fixes

Tiles provide an easy-clean, hardwearing wall surface for kitchens, bathrooms and utility areas. Although tiles are reasonably durable, they are not indestructible. Accidents can happen: occasionally a tile can crack, chip or break, grout can discolor and seals can deteriorate, spoiling the appearance of your room.

283 How to replace a broken wall tile

Hopefully you will have a few spare tiles at the ready. This isn't a difficult job, but the challenge is removing the damaged tile without causing more damage to its neighbors. When the tile is in place, re-grout following Steps 1–2 of "TLC for tiles: re-grouting" (opposite).

YOU WILL NEED
- Grout rake
- Drill and ceramic bit
- Protective gloves
- Protective goggles
- Chisel
- Hammer
- Scraper
- Spare tiles
- Tile adhesive
- Grout spreader
- Tile spacers (if necessary)
- Wooden batten
- Grout

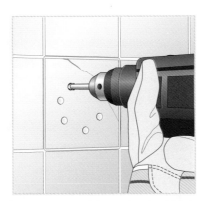

1. Loosen the grout around the edges of the damaged tile using a grout rake. Now drill a few holes in the tile surface with an electric drill and a ceramic bit. Be sure to wear gloves and protective goggles to protect against sharp ceramic shards.

2. Place the tip of a chisel in the center of the tile and tap firmly with a hammer. This should break up the tile a little more, allowing easy removal. Chip out the broken pieces, working away from the center until the tile is removed and the tile bed is clean. Be careful not to gouge the wall surface underneath.

3. Use a metal scraper to remove any old tile adhesive from the tile bed and to clean all four edges. Any lumps of dry grout or adhesive will keep the new tile from lying flush with its neighbors, and will spoil the finish of the tiled field. Insert the dry tile and test for a good fit.

4. Apply new adhesive to the back of the replacement tile using the grout spreader, and place it in position. If the tile does not have spacing lugs, insert tile spacers into the gaps on all four sides to ensure an even space between it and the neighboring tiles. Tamp the tile flush with the rest using a wooden batten. Allow the adhesive to dry before re-grouting.

FIX IT

Making repairs without spares

If you don't have any spares or are just making a repair to existing tilework, you may have difficulty finding a match. Think about replacing a few extra ones and introducing a contrasting pattern rather than having one odd one in the field.

284 TLC for tiles: re-grouting

Grout can discolor and spoil the appearance of a tiled area. If your tiles are still sound and in good condition it is an easy – though very labor-intensive – task to remove and replace the old grout. It is worth trying cleaning methods first, but if the grout is still looking worn and grubby then replacing it is the answer. It really will make a difference – grotty grout looks so unsightly.

YOU WILL NEED
- Grout rake
- Grout spreader
- Grout
- Damp sponge

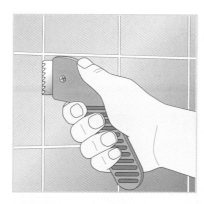

1. Use the hardened serrated blade of a grout rake to remove the old grout to about half the depth of the tile. Work methodically, removing the vertical grout lines first, then the horizontal ones. This is hard work so take plenty of breaks; you will certainly get a bicep workout!

2. Use the rubber blade of a grout spreader to squeeze the new grout into the spaces between each tile, working in diagonal sweeps to keep the grout from lifting out again. When complete, use a damp sponge to remove excess grout and to clean the tile surface. Rinse the sponge frequently with clean water to avoid leaving cloudy residue on the tile surface. Run a wet fingertip or a grout finisher over the lines to give a neat profile.

285 Replacing sealant

Flexible silicone sealant does a good job of keeping out water very well when it is complete; however, the sealant tends to deteriorate over time and can break and allow water to seep behind the tiles – into gaps between fixtures and the wall. Simply peel off the entire seal, and clean any residue or grime that may have collected along the edges. Make sure all surfaces are dry, and then apply more using a cartridge of sealant and a cartridge gun (see page 75 for method). It is best to replace the whole seal rather than sections, because the joins will be noticeable.

286 Clean-up shortcut

Apply car wax to tiles before setting them in place – this makes it easier to clean away grout residue when the job is finished.

287 Short-term whitening

Try using a grout reviver pen. Scrub the grout clean with warm water and detergent, and when dry, whiten the discolored grout using the reviver pen. It's not a permanent fix but will provide a quick facelift.

TRY IT

Cleaning grimey grout

If you don't have time to re-grout, try using a grout-cleaning product as a quick fix. Minor staining can be removed and black mold growth inhibited. Simply apply the product according to the manufacturer's instructions. Clean each grout line with an old toothbrush. Rinse well and let dry.

FIXING PAINT JOB KNOW-HOW

* *

HOW TO TOUCH UP PAINTED WALLS

288 Your lovely new paint finish can easily be spoiled by dirt and grime caused by everyday wear and tear. Some marks can be cleaned off, but others will have to be obliterated with a light touch-up, especially in high-traffic areas. Follow this sequence to ensure the mark disappears and you won't notice the repair. Note: Always repair dents and cracks before touching up paint job.

✳ **YOU WILL NEED**
• Dust sheets
• Decorator's tape
• Small amount of the same paint
• Saucer
• Small artist's paintbrush
• Narrow paintbrush
• Paint roller
• Roller tray

1. Move all furniture away from the surface to be retouched, and use dust sheets to protect the floor and furnishings. Use decorator's tape to mask off moldings, base boards, door and window frames, and sockets and switches.

2. Decant some paint onto a saucer if using a brush or a roller tray if using a roller. Apply paint to the marked area. Work from the center outward and feather the paint by lightening your touch the closer you get to the outer edge. This will disguise the join between the touched-up patch and the rest.

3. If the touched-up patch has highlighted that the rest of the wall is shabby, you may just have to do the whole wall to avoid a patchy finish. (Consider just painting one wall from corner to corner rather than the whole room.)

4. Touch-up jobs work best on recently painted walls. Paint can fade with exposure to sunlight and a patch of identical paint can show up quite obviously.

5. Try to work in good light so you can see exactly what you're doing. Marks and scuffs at eye level can be hard to disguise successfully.

Quick tips for touch-ups

• Use a small blob of toothpaste on a soft cloth to remove scuff marks from painted surfaces.

• A small artist's paintbrush is handy for very small touch-up jobs. Dip the tip into the paint and stipple gently on the surface to disguise the marks.

• Sponge paintbrushes are good for touch-ups; they don't leave brush marks and are disposable.

• Cotton swabs are a good way to touch up very small spots.

290

HOW TO TOUCH UP PAINTED MOLDINGS, DOORS AND WINDOW FRAMES

289 Paint with a gloss finish can also get stained, damaged or chipped, resulting in unsightly patches where the subsurface or primer shows through. As the paint layer on doors, windows and moldings tends to be slightly thicker than on walls, you will require a slightly different method.

✳ **YOU WILL NEED**
• Brush
• Sandpaper
• Paintbrush
• Primer
• Paint
• Wood filler

1. Do not apply paint directly onto a chip. There will be a noticeable ridge where the old paint ends and the new paint starts.

2. Brush away loose paint particles, and then use sandpaper to rub over the areas lightly to create a key on the surrounding surfaces.

3. Apply primer to bare wood if it is exposed, or apply a thin paint layer if you can see the primer underneath. Let dry.

4. Run your fingers over the chipped area to see if you can feel a ridge; reapply more primer or paint, and let it dry.

5. Finally, apply the topcoat with a small brush, working outward from the center of the damaged area. Feather the edge of the fresh paint to minimize the join between old and new paint.

Note: First apply wood filler to deep gouges, scrapes or dents. Let dry, and then use sandpaper to rub smooth. Now apply primer to the filled area; if you apply paint directly over filler, the repair will show through as a dull spot.

What can go wrong with paint?

291 Lots of things can happen to the surface of paint, and, unfortunately, the only answer is to rub down and repaint. However, it helps to know the causes of the problem so that you can keep it from recurring.

292 ## Keep some matching paint

Before trying to cover up any surface blemishes on your paint job, make sure you have some spare paint from the original job or the color and shade code so you can purchase some more. Never try to guess a color match; the touched-up patch will stick out like a sore thumb.

PROBLEM	CAUSE	FIX
Flaking	Paint applied over a damp or powdery surface.	More thorough surface preparation is required.
Crazing	Topcoat applied over undercoat that was still damp.	Be sure to allow adequate drying time between coats.
Blistering	Moisture or resins trapped between surface and paint coat are drawn out by heat.	Always ensure that the surface is completely dry before paint application.
Curtaining	Thick runs or sagging paint film caused by very thick application of paint on vertical surfaces.	Do not apply paint too thickly – two thin coats are better than one thick coat.
Cratering	Rain or condensation droplets can cause pits or craters in the paint surface.	Make sure to do your painting on a dry day and in a well-ventilated area.
Wrinkling	Paint can wrinkle if applied too thickly on a horizontal surface.	Do not apply paint too thickly – two thin coats are better than one thick coat.

Using old paint

293 If you have kept leftover paint then touch-ups will be easy. However, there are certain pitfalls to avoid when reopening paint cans.

✳ Always clean dust and dirt away from the lid before opening. Particles can drop into the paint and be transferred to your surface.

✳ Pry off paint lids carefully using a flat screwdriver or paint lid popping key to avoid damaging the can.

✳ If the paint can has been undisturbed for a long while, invert it and rest it on the lid for about 20 minutes before opening. Turn the can the right way up, and then open.

✳ Stir the paint thoroughly with a stirring stick or dowel before using. You could even take it back to the store it came from and ask the staff to shake it with their electric stirrer to make sure it is fully blended.

✳ Decant the paint into a clean saucer or paint roller tray. If you're using equipment that has been undisturbed for a time, then there could be a dust or dirt buildup on receptacles. Be sure they're really clean before you use them.

✳ Make sure the previously used brushes or rollers are clean, dry and free from dust, dirt and grease.

✳ Apply paint sparingly to touch-up areas. It's better to apply another coat than apply paint one coat too thickly.

✳ It's a good idea to decant leftover paint into a smaller container. If you have a small amount of paint left in a large can, by the time you need to use it a thick skin may have formed on the surface and you might not have much usable paint left. Glass jam jars or screw-top preserving jars are a good size.

✳ Always label new containers clearly for future reference – record the paint name, manufacturer's name, color code and finish. The name of the store you bought it from can be useful too if it was a custom mix.

What to do in an emergency

It's really useful to know where the household gas, electricity and water meter controls are in your home in case there's an emergency – you may need to turn off their power while decorating. Keep a notebook with all the details handy, just in case you forget or need to inform someone else.

Safety note: If in doubt, call a professional. Never tamper with household utility supplies if you are unsure what to do.

294 Your home record

Essential service control locations:

- Inside/outside water stop tap and meter
- Valves on supply from cold-water tank
- Isolating valves on appliance supply pipes (toilets, baths, etc.)
- Drain mechanisms for sealed units (heating systems, etc.)
- Main on/off switch for gas supply and meter
- Isolating valves on appliance pipes
- Main on/off switch for electricity supply and meter
- Household circuit breaker switches for electrical appliances
- Heating programmer

295 Fuses

- Older homes often have fuses instead of circuit breakers. Keep some spare fuses of the correct size handy in case one blows.
- If just one circuit has blown, disconnect the appliance that has caused the overload before changing the fuse.
- Shut off the household supply before changing a fuse.

296 Meter key

If your meter is enclosed in a protective housing the chances are that you'll need a key like this to open it. The triangular hole in the shaft engages with a simple closing mechanism to open and close the access door. They can be made of plastic or metal.

297 Circuit breakers

- The main circuit breaker, usually located inside the main panel at the top, shuts off all of the electricity to the house. In an emergency, this is the one to turn off. Otherwise, shut off only the branch circuit breaker that serves the problem circuit – that way, other parts of your house will continue to have lights and power. The main circuit breaker does not shut off the wires that run from the main panel breakers to the electric meter – these are always hot (electrically charged).

- Each switch relates to a specific circuit. If a circuit switch has tripped due to an overload (by an appliance on that circuit), disconnect the suspect appliance, and reset the switch by turning it off and on again.
- When you open the main panel's cover, be sure there are no exposed electrical wires except for an exposed (non-insulated) solid copper ground wire. A protective panel should conceal all wiring – only the breakers or fuses should be exposed.

- If this is not the case, call an electrician to have your electrical panel made safe. Touching the wrong wire or bare metal contact in an exposed electrical panel can electrocute you. Never touch bare metal contacts inside a disconnect panel.
- If you experience regular problems call an experienced professional. Do not attempt repairs or investigation yourself.

298 Electricity

Lots of home-decorating jobs will require the power to be turned off, with painting or wallpapering around light switches and power sockets being the most common. Your home may have fused or circuit-breaker panels, and a household on/off switch for the entire supply.

Where?
- Most power supply units are easily accessible, though you may need a flashlight or a ladder. May be located in basements or utility rooms.

How?
- A clearly labeled on/off switch will identify the main power shut-off. This will shut off the entire supply.
- Separate circuit-breaker switches will switch off different circuits, e.g., lights, sockets, etc. These are usually labeled.
- Your supply may have fuses or circuit breakers (see left); always be prepared and have suitable spares.

When?
- In an emergency, turn off the entire power supply.
- You may need to turn off the power supply when decorating, or when an electrician is installing new appliances or repairing your electrical circuits.
- If a certain circuit has blown, you may need to reset the circuit switch.

299 Gas supply

Shutting off the gas supply during home-decoration tasks is something of a rarity. Still, it is best to know where the supply is and what to do just in case you need to act quickly in an emergency. Note: If you have turned off the gas, do not turn it on again yourself; this must be done by a professional.

Where?
- The meter may be located inside your home, on an outside wall or in a basement.
- The shut-off valve is usually located next to the meter; if the valve is parallel to the supply pipe then it is open and the supply is on.

How?
- Your home will have a gas meter with an on/off lever that you may have to engage with an adjustable wrench.
- Keep a wrench close to the meter, just in case.
- Using the wrench, turn the valve so it lies perpendicular to the supply pipe, and in the off/closed position.
- Make a note of the dial numbers when you turn off the supply, and check a little later to see if they have changed to ensure the supply is really off.

When?
- You smell gas or suspect a leak.
- When closing up your home for an extended vacation.

300 Water supply

It is less common to turn off the water during a home-decorating project; however, if you are unfortunate enough to drive a nail through a water pipe, knowing where the shut-off valve is and how to do it quickly will be extremely valuable.

Where?
- Look for the water meter, usually located in the utility room or basement close to where the household supply enters your home.
- Individual fixtures have supply cut-off valves located on the supply pipe.

- Bathtubs or fixtures with enclosed pipework will have a removable access panel; the shut-off valve will be found inside.
- Sometimes individual shut-off valves are concealed under floorboards.

How?
- The main water valve is closed by turning it in a clockwise direction.
- Individual fixtures have their own shut-off valves, operated with a handle or screw that can be engaged with a screwdriver.

When?
- If disaster strikes and you have a leak.
- If you have accidentally damaged a water supply pipe.
- If a plumber or tradesman is carrying out installation or repairs for you.

Hiring a professional

If you decide that it will not be your hands clutching that paintbrush, you need to hire someone to do the work for you.

Reasons to take this option might include:

- You know that doing the job right can't be achieved in the time you have available.

- You don't want to spend hours in home stores finding the right equipment and materials.

- You don't have the right painting and decorating skills and don't feel confident about taking on a major project. Maybe you don't know where to go for materials and equipment or how to use them for creating certain effects.

- You don't know what you want. You need someone to help you develop your style.

- You have lots of ideas but are not sure if they would work and need someone to advise you and perhaps prepare room layouts so that you can see what they would look like. Or you may have a few ideas about individual rooms, but you haven't got the overall plan that will ensure a coherent scheme throughout your home.

- Your home dates from a particular period and you need advice about period colors and details.

You have a choice: paint and wallpaper contractor or interior designer. If you have a really clear idea of what you want, roughly what the materials will cost and where most of the supplies will come from, go for a contractor. You don't need imaginative input from a contractor – you just want your plan carried out to a professional standard. If you would like creative input, it's probably an interior designer that you need. The table below will help you decide who it is you should hire.

Finding and briefing a paint and wallpaper contractor

A contractor could be a single person or a small team. They are going to be in your house for a while, and their work is going to be in your home for considerably longer, so you need to feel confident in them and their abilities. Anyone can call themselves professional, so it's important to bear in mind the following pointers when deciding on the right one for the job:

- Ask for recommendations from friends or other local service providers.

- Consult a trade association for reliable professionals. The Painting and Decorating Contractors of America (PDCA) is a trade organization, but membership is voluntary.

- Look in local newspapers and on community websites for advertisements and recommendations.

- When meeting with a potential contractor, ask for references from previous customers and follow them up. A true professional won't mind this at all.

Pros and cons of hiring a professional

	CAN DO	CAN'T DO	ADVANTAGES	DISADVANTAGES
Paint and wallpaper contractor	All the practical interior decoration.	Decide or advise on your scheme.	Less expensive than a designer; offer all the do-it-yourself skills that you may be lacking.	Limited design input; will need overseeing by you.
Interior designer	Give you new ideas; supply labor; check technical details such as electrical safety.		Will create a design scheme; will manage contractors.	More expensive; the result may bear his or her hallmark more than yours unless you can communicate your ideas during the planning.

- Meet up a couple of times before offering the job. Feel confident that you can work with this person. He or she doesn't have to be your best friend, but you do need to feel you can be straightforward and honest with them.

- Ask for an estimate of what the job will cost and how long it will take.

- There's no substitute for a clear and agreed written brief, setting out the tasks to be completed.

Finding and briefing an interior designer

Take note of the advice above for finding a paint and wallpaper contractor, but in addition:

- If you've seen an interior you really like, ask who designed it and get in touch with that person.

- Only approach designers who work on residential projects – many of them specialize in offices, stores, public buildings or other areas.

- In the US and Canada, most interior designers will have a qualification recognized by the National Council for Interior Design (NCID).

- You may want to check whether your designer is a member of a trade organization, such as the American Society of Interior Designers (ASID), the Interior Designers of Canada or the Foundation for Interior Design Educational Research (IDEC).

- When talking to a potential designer, be clear what it is you need both from them and from the scheme itself.

- Be upfront about your budget, and stick to it. If it becomes apparent that your budget will not stretch to what you want to achieve, you may need to rethink your plan or spread out the work over a longer period of time.

- Create an electronic Pinterest board with swatches and photographs to show fabrics, patterns, effects and colors you like.

- Decide what furniture you want to keep, and list it.

- Consider how you feel about room layouts and whether you want to keep them as they are or alter them.

- Be prepared for a dialogue. Part of a designer's expertise is in adapting your ideas into a practical scheme; that is what you are paying for.

Costs and project management

Whomever you choose, be clear when conveying your ideas, and check the work as it goes along. If you are paying an hourly or daily rate rather than a flat fee, it is especially important that you do this efficiently, because indecision and lack of clarity soak up time, which will cost money.

- Agree whether you are to pay a flat fee, a day rate or by the hour. Get this in writing.

- Agree what you will pay for, such as materials.

Will you cover expenses?

- Your budget must include a contingency for unexpected costs.

- Agree when you will make payments. It is reasonable for professionals to have some money up front to pay for materials and disbursements, and for some of the fee to be held back until all the work is complete and satisfactory.

- Agree to a detailed plan, and then set up regular meetings to make sure everyone is sticking to it. These might be once or twice a week, depending on the length of the project.

Useful terminology

Access equipment Ladders, platforms, scaffolding and any other equipment used to reach high, inaccessible areas.

Aggregate Sand and small stone, which is mixed with cement and water to form concrete.

Architrave The molding that frames a door or window opening.

Baluster A post (one of a set) used to support a handrail along an open staircase.

Balustrade The complete barrier installed along open staircases and landings. It consists of the balusters, newels and handrail.

Base board A wood molding used horizontally along the walls where they meet the floor.

Batten A thin strip of wood, typically of 2 in x 1 in (50 mm x 25 mm) softwood.

Bead or Beading A type of molding that has a half round or more intricate profile. It's often used for edging and as decoration.

Bevel A surface that meets another surface at an angle of less than 90 degrees.

Bind When a door or hinged casement rubs against its surrounding frame.

Bore To drill a hole greater than about ½ in (13 mm) in diameter.

Butt To fit together two pieces of material side by side or edge to edge.

Carcass The box-like, five-sided structure that forms the base of certain types of furniture such as a kitchen cupboard or chest of drawers.

Caulk A flexible compound used to seal a joint between two surfaces, such as a wall and base board, where a degree of movement is expected.

Chair rail A decorative molding installed on walls about waist height, originally to prevent furniture from marring the walls.

Chamfer A narrow, angled surface, often at 45 degrees, running along the corner of a piece such as a beam or post.

Concave A surface that curves inward.

Contour The outline or shape of an object.

Convex A surface that curves outward.

Cornice A decorative molding fixed at the junction between the walls and ceiling, often used to hide cracks.

Countersink A tapered recess made in the top section of a screw hole to allow the head of the screw to sit flush with the surface of the material.

Crown molding A prefabricated concave molding, often used as a cornice.

Cutting-in brush A type of brush with bristles cut on an angle to assist painting neatly at an edge such as at a cornice or architrave.

Damp-proof course Also referred to as DPC, an impervious material laid in the building foundation to prevent moisture from the ground spreading to the walls of the building.

Damp-proof membrane Also referred to as DPM, an impervious material laid under a concrete floor to prevent moisture seeping through it.

Dowel A small cylindrical wooden peg, sometimes with grooves running the length of its surface. It can be used to plug holes or to form a joint by inserting it into holes in two pieces of wood.

Eggshell paint A paint that dries with a low-sheen or low-gloss finish.

End grain The fibers in the end of the wood exposed after cutting across the wood.

Feather To dull or taper an edge to make it less noticeable, a technique often used in sanding and painting.

Fillet A small, often wooden, piece of molding with a square cross-section.

Furring strip Thin length of wood fixed in parallel strips across a wall or ceiling, forming a framework to which cladding is attached.

Glazing point or sprig A small triangular-shaped piece of metal for holding a pane of window glass in a rabbet.

Gloss paint A solvent-based paint that dries with a hard, shiny finish. It's suitable for painting interior and exterior wood and metal. This type of paint needs a longer drying time and is difficult to clean off paint equipment.

Grain The direction of the fibers in a piece of wood.

Grout A water-resistant paste used to seal the gaps between ceramic or other similar tiles fixed to walls or floors.

Hardwood Wood that comes from broad-leaved – usually deciduous – trees such as ash, beech and oak. This type of wood is typically hard; however, balsa is classified as a hardwood but it is a soft, lightweight material.

Head The highest horizontal member of a window or door frame.

Head plate The highest horizontal component of a stud partition wall.

Jamb The vertical side member of the frame that surrounds a door or window.

Joist A horizontal wood or steel beam used to support a heavy structure such as a floor or ceiling.

Kerf The groove created in a material when cut by any type of saw.

Key To roughen a surface, often by sanding, to provide a better grip for a material such as paint or adhesive.

Latex paint Used on interior walls and ceilings, a water-based paint with a matte or sheen finish. It dries quickly and is easy to clean off paint equipment.

Matte finish A nonreflective finish on a material such as paint or quarry tiles.

Miter A joint between two beveled pieces to form an angle, often a 45-degree angle.

Molding A narrow, usually decorative, strip of wood or other material. It is available shaped in different profiles. Base boards and chair and picture rails are types of molding.

Mortise A rectangular-shaped recess cut into wood. It may be used to form a joint by combining it with a tenoned end. Alternatively, it is used to hold a striker plate in a door frame for a lock or latch.

Mullion A vertical dividing component of a window.

Muntin A vertical component between panels; they are used to form a paneled door or wall paneling.

Newel Part of the balustrade; the wider post at both the top and bottom of a staircase for supporting the handrail.

Nogging A short horizontal component between studs in a partition wall.

Nosing The front, often rounded, edge of a stair tread.

Pare To use a chisel, bevel side up, to remove fine shavings from wood – often done to smooth a surface from which wood was removed.

Pattern repeat The distance of a motif before it begins to be duplicated, or repeated.

Pelmet A decorative wood unit used to hide the top edge of curtains or a structure such as the track of a sliding door.

Picture rail A type of decorative molding that is normally fixed horizontally to the walls above head height.

Pile The fabrics raised from a backing – often used to classify a type of carpet.

Pilot hole A hole drilled in a material to guide a screw. It should be smaller in diameter than the shank of the screw without its threads.

Plinth A four-sided base on which a structure, such as a cupboard, is placed.

Primer A liquid substance used to seal a material, such as plaster, drywall, wood or metal, before applying an undercoat.

Profile The contour or outline of an object.

Proud When an object protrudes from the surface.

Rabbet A step-shaped recess in the edge of a work piece, often as part of a joint but also used for exterior door frames to prevent the door from swinging through.

Rail The horizontal piece of wood that joins vertical pieces in a frame or carcass.

Raised grain When the wood's surface is roughened by damping, which causes its fibers to swell.

Reveal The vertical side of a window or door opening.

Riser The vertical component of a step or stair.

Sash The structure of a window that holds the glass. It usually opens, either up and down or sideways, but it is sometimes fixed.

Scarf A joint between two pieces of material cut at matching angles – unlike a miter, the faces of the pieces are flush.

Score A line that marks a division or boundary, or the act of making the line.

Scribe To mark a line with a pointed tool, or to copy the profile of a surface onto a piece of material that will be trimmed to butt against the surface.

Secret nailing A method of securing components together, such as tongue-and-groove floorboards, using fixings at an angle and punched below the surface of the work piece.

Sheen finish Also known as a silk finish, the amount of reflectiveness of a painted or other surface, midway between matte and gloss finishes.

Shim A thin piece of material, such cardboard or plywood, used to as packing to fill a gap between materials.

Sill The lowest horizontal component of a window or door frame or of a stud partition wall.

Size A thin gelatinous solution used to seal a surface, such as a plaster wall, prior to hanging wallpaper.

Softwood Wood that comes from coniferous trees, including cedar. Although typically soft in nature, yew is one type that is hard.

Sole plate Also called a stud partition sill, the lowest horizontal member of a wood-frame partition wall.

Spandrel The triangular material used to fill the space below an outside stringer on a staircase.

Staff bead The innermost strip of wood that holds a sash that moves up and down in the window frame.

Stain A liquid that changes the color of wood but does not protect it. It comes in water-based and oil-based versions.

Stile A vertical side component of a window sash or door.

Straight edge A length of either metal or wood that has at least one true straight edge. It is often used for marking straight lines or making a surface level.

Stringer or String One of a pair of boards that runs along the staircase, from one floor to another, supporting the treads and risers. If against a wall, it's called an inside stringer; if there is an open side, it's an outside stringer.

Stud A vertical member of a wood-frame wall.

Stud partition wall A wall constructed with a wood frame, usually covered with drywall.

Subsidence The sinking of the ground that occurs where land has been infilled or when it becomes excessively dry and shrinks. This may be due to a drought or to a large tree.

Sugar soap or Trisodium phosphate A strong, alkaline-based liquid that is used for cleaning painted and other types of surfaces.

Template Paper, card, metal or other sheet material formed in a specific shape or pattern to be used as a guide for transferring the shape to the work piece.

Tenon A projecting end of a wood component that fits into a mortise to form a joint.

Tongue and groove A joint between two pieces of material – such as floorboards or cladding – in which one piece has a projecting edge that fits into a slot or groove on the edge of the other piece.

Topcoat The last coat of a finish applied to a surface. There may be several coats underneath it.

Tread The horizontal part of a step that is walked on.

Undercoat One or more layers of a paint or varnish to cover a primer or build up a protective finish before applying a topcoat.

Underlay A layer of material to provide a smooth surface for laying a decorative flooring. Rubber, felt or paper may be used under carpeting; hardboard or plywood may be used for other types of flooring.

Utility knife Also referred to as a trimming knife or Stanley knife, a handle that holds a replacable blade, which may or may not retract.

Varnish A liquid applied to wood materials, it hardens to form a protective surface. It may be clear or colored.

Veneer A thin decorative layer of wood applied to a less attractive surface.

Wet-and-dry abrasive paper A paper with silicon carbide attached for smoothing surfaces. It may be used wet.

Index

Index

2900

Credits

Quarto would like to thank the following agencies and manufacturers for supplying images for inclusion in this book:

Albo003, Shutterstock.com, p.39bc
AlexAvich, Shutterstock.com, p.17br
Alexeysun, Shutterstock.com, p.118b
All door handles and hooks, Shutterstock.com, pp.134–135
All images, Sutterstock.com, p.15b
Amat, Aaron, Shutterstock.com, p.137br
Amby, Thomas, Shutterstock.com, p.118t
Andresr, Shutterstock.com, pp.2cr, 30
Andrew, Mayovskyy, Shutterstock.com, p.17bc
Anteromite, Shutterstock.com, p.14t
Archiwiz, Shutterstock.com, p.14b
Artazum and Iriana Shiyan, Shutterstock.com, pp.2bc, 119bl
Audioscience, Shutterstock.com, p.37b
B&Q, www.diy.com, p.128b
Bezmaski, Shutterstock.com, p15cr
Bilic, Nikola, Shutterstock.com, p.127tr
Boyko, Yuriy, Shutterstock.com, All images p.16t
Chinsai, Warut, Shutterstock.com, p.163br
Cole, Matthew, Shutterstock.com, p.44t
Coprid, Shutterstock.com, p.39bl
Craven Dunnill, available through www.cravendunnill.co.uk, pp.78t/c, 79tl/tc/tr/bl/br, 75–76
Crepesoles, Shutterstock.com, p.23tr
Didden, Shutterstock.com, p.26b
Divizia, Claudio, Shutterstock.com, p.19tr
Dodge, Christopher, Shutterstock.com, p.39ctr
Donatas1205, Shutterstock.com, p.14b
Dudaeva, Shutterstock.com, p.39tcr
Dulux, pp.2cl, 31t, 53t, 92b, 95t/b, 108t, 154
Farrow & Ball, www.farrow-ball.com, pp.10, 31b, 40, 113tl/bl
Fornasar, Giulio, Shutterstock.com, p.20bc
Gavran333, Shutterstock.com, p.14cl
GeniusKp, Shutterstock.com, p.37r
GoodMood Photo, Shutterstock.com, p.2tl
Graham & Brown, available through www.grahambrown.com, pp.2bl, 3tr/bl/br, 32–33, 34–35, 50–51, 52t/b, 53b, 64, 93t, 106, 107t/br, 109b, 116, 144r

Gresei, Shutterstock.com, p.16c
Gudella, Peter, Shutterstock.com, p.56t
Hofmeester, Patricia, Shutterstock.com, p.163cr
Hsagencia, Shutterstock.com, p.20br
Humbak, Shutterstock.com, p22tcr
Ibragimov, Maxim, p.13b
Indigolotos, Shutterstock.com, pp.13, 111cl
Irin-k, Shutterstock.com, p.3tl
Irina, Tischenko, Shutterstock.com, p15t
Ispace, Shutterstock.com, p.111cbl
Kellis, Shutterstock.com, p.160br
Kitch Bain, Shutterstock.com, p.39tl
Konuk, Levent, Shutterstock.com, p12tl
Koosen, Shutterstock.com, p.14tb
Kosev, Alex, Shutterstock.com, p.13tr
Kostsov, Shutterstock.com, p.151bl
Kovalchuk, Igor, Shutterstock.com, p.16br
Kozini, Shutterstock.com, p.111b
Ktynzq, Shutterstock.com, p.167t
Liveshot, Shutterstock.com, p.120br
Malyshev, Petr, Shutterstock.com, p.16b
Maxx-Studio, Shutterstock.com, p.15cr
Mediagram, Shutterstock.com, p.82b
Mihalec, Shutterstock.com, p.12cl
Minakani, available through www.minakani.com, p.108bl/br
Mrsiraphol, Shutterstock.com, p.22t
Neamov, Shutterstock.com, p.12cr
Oksana2010, Shutterstock.com, p26t
Oleksandr Chub, Shutterstock.com, p.39tr
Olivier Le Moal, Shutterstock.com, p.3tc
Papa1266, Shutterstock.com, p.39cl
Pogson, Norman, Shutterstock.com, p.18c
Popov, Andrey, Shutterstock.com, p.12tl
Potapova, Valerie, Shutterstock.com, p.119br
Ristevski, Filip, Shutterstock.com, p.17bl
Roberaten, Shutterstock.com, p.44bl
Robinson, Leena, Shutterstock.com, p.158ctl
Sagitov, Oleksii, Shutterstock.com, pp.23cl, 62
Savitskiy, Lev, Shutterstock.com, p.20t
SeDmi, Shutterstock.com, p.63c
Sergio Foto, Shutterstock.com, p.26bt
Srdjan111, Shutterstock.com, p.66bl
Staroseltsev, Alex, Shutterstock.com, p.27cr
Swoon, Shutterstock.com, p.2tc
Terekhov Igor, Shutterstock.com, p.19t
Thanom, Shutterstock.com, p.39br

The Binary Box, available through http://thebinarybox.co.uk, p.107bl
Timages, Shutterstock.com, p.20bl
The Tool & Gauge Company (UK) Limited T/A www.diytools.com, pp.18b, 19cr, 20cr/cbr, 21c/cl/c, 22bl, 23ctr/cr/bcr, 26bcl/bct/bc/bctr, 39c (6), 59btl, 71bl, 86cr, 115cl, 121br, 163bl
Topseller, Shutterstock.com, p.11, 84t
Vader, Julie, Shutterstock.com, p.44br
Vinyl Impression, available through www.vinylimpression.co.uk, p.109t
Vinzstudio, Shutterstock.com, p.82tr
Vlabo, Shutterstock.com, p.59b
VOJTa Herout, Shutterstock.com, p.2tr
Yanas, Shutterstock.com, p12b
Yevgeniy, Steshkin, Shutterstock.com, p.158cbl
YK, Shutterstock.com, p.15ct

Courtesy of "Black & Decker Here's How Painting", pp.83tl/tr/bc/br, 85tl/tr/bl/br, 89btl/br/bl, 115, 130tr,
Courtesy of "Black & Decker The Complete Photo Guide to Home Decorating Projects", pp.83bl, 112cr/bc/br, 120tl/tr/bl/br, 124bl, 125tl/tr/bl/br,

All step-by-step and other images are the copyright of Quarto Publishing plc. While every effort has been made to credit contributors, Quarto would like to apologize should there have been any omissions or errors — and would be pleased to make the appropriate correction for future editions of the book.